Marijuana

Marijuana

What's a Parent to Believe?

Timmen L. Cermak, M.D.

 HAZELDEN®

Hazelden
Center City, Minnesota 55012-0176

1-800-328-0094
1-651-213-4590 (Fax)
www.hazelden.org

ISBN: 1-59285-039-1

Author's note
The vignettes in this book are composites of actual situations. Any resemblance to specific persons, living or dead, or specific events is purely coincidental.

Excerpt from *From Chocolate to Morphine*, copyright © 1983, 1993 by Andrew Weil and Winifred Rosen, reprinted with permission of Houghton Mifflin Company, all rights reserved.

The framework for "Why Kids Use Alcohol and Other Drugs" from the pamphlet *Facts about Kids' Use of Alcohol and Other Drugs* by David Wilmes ©1991 is reprinted with permission of the author.

The Twelve Steps of Marijuana Anonymous are reprinted with the permission of Marijuana Anonymous World Services. Permission to reprint the Twelve Steps does not mean that MA has reviewed or approved the contents of this publication, nor that MA agrees with the views expressed herein. (Although the Twelve Steps of MA are patterned after the Twelve Steps of Alcoholics Anonymous, with permission, the two programs are not affiliated.)

The Twelve Steps of Marijuana Anonymous (MA), as adapted by MA with permission of Alcoholics Anonymous World Services, Inc. (AAWS), are reprinted with permission of MA and AAWS. The Twelve Steps of Alcoholics Anonymous are reprinted with the permission of AAWS. AAWS's permission to reprint the foregoing material does not mean that AAWS has reviewed or approved the contents of this publication, or that AAWS necessarily agrees with the views expressed herein. Alcoholics Anonymous is a program of recovery from alcoholism *only*—use or permissible adaptation of AA's Twelve Steps in connection with programs and activities which are patterned after AA, but which address other problems, or in any other non-AA context, does not imply otherwise.

07 06 05 04 03   6 5 4 3 2 1

Cover design by David Spohn
Interior design by David Spohn
Typesetting by Tursso Companies

To my brother, Laird Scott Cermak, who built a great career on looking for the evidence

Contents

Illustrations

Acknowledgments

Stephanie Brown, Ph.D., had the biggest impact on my career, opening my interest in chemical dependence, including the impact of addiction on family issues and children of alcoholics. Her insightful supervision throughout my psychiatric residency helped integrate mental health and addiction perspectives from the very beginning of my formal training. Many others have added valuable lessons along the way, but the basic framework she provided is still with me as part of the scaffolding I stand upon in whatever contributions I have to offer.

Karl Pribram, M.D., also had a fundamental impact on my thinking, deepening my comprehension of the brain. His challenging guidance of my postdoctoral fellowship helped integrate neurophysiology and psychology, the brain and the mind, into a seamless unity. He helped ground my perspective firmly in the physical world without detracting from the humanistic elements that emerge and create such richness and depth in our lives.

The California Society of Addiction Medicine, and particularly those members who made up the ad hoc Task Force on Medical Marijuana (Doctors William Brostoff, Nicola Longmuir, Joe McCarthy, Tod Mykuriya, Max Schneider, David Smith, and Tom Ungerleiter), provided invaluable checks and balances in writing the background papers CSAM used for developing public positions regarding cannabis. They supplied the perspective needed to find the middle ground amid data contributed by hundreds of researchers.

Roger Lake, an enduring colleague, constantly challenged me with his systemic perspective. Consultations with him keep my view of patients fresh and unsettled.

Dan Baum, author of the excellent history of America's drug war *Smoke and Mirrors*, provided practical advice on how to craft a book to a particular audience. I am grateful for his rescuing me from the grandiosity of thinking I could interest everyone in what fascinates me.

Andrew Weil, author of *The Natural Mind* and *From Chocolate to Morphine*, modeled for me how medical rigor can be combined with common sense. I am grateful for his contributions to my thinking, especially for demonstrating how strong personal views do not prevent one from developing balanced understanding.

Karen Chernyaev, the Hazelden editor who worked with me from the first concept for this book to its final form, has contributed in ways that will be transparent to most readers. She has extraordinary skill at combining tough demands for clarity and consistency with just the right amount of praise and encouragement to soothe the sting to my pride. I am very grateful for how hard she has worked to make me look good. Anyone who saw the first draft would understand the extent of her contribution.

My family has provided immense forbearance, as every author's relatives must. Their permission to discuss our mutual history is a gift to me and all readers. I appreciate their patience, especially during the final months of lost evenings and weekends. Special thanks to my wife and colleague, Mary, who has read multiple drafts and given me another valuable pair of eyes to see what worked and what was too opaque to be shown to anyone else. Her comments were immensely helpful.

Gary Kent and John Mercer, at the Mission Mountain School, contributed by teaching me important lessons about adolescents, the last psychological frontier I had to cross. Their commonsense approach is refreshing, and I liked the horses, too.

I especially want to acknowledge those who have taught me the most—the decades of patients who have painstakingly described the most minute aspects of their experience with alcohol and other drugs. By listening carefully, I learned that everyone has his or her own individual experience of marijuana even while commonalities run through their experiences, as well. It has been a privilege to be taken into their confidence. I hope this book does justice to their trust in me and that I have given them a tenth of what they have given me.

I write to music and wish to acknowledge recordings that have been instrumental in keeping my mind on task: the soundtracks from *The Power of One*, *Dead Man Walking*, and *Rabbit-Proof Fence*, the Blind Boys of Alabama, Ladysmith Black Mambazo, Moby, John Michael Talbot, Bob Marley's *Legend*, and Meatloaf (for the times I was most frustrated).

Finally, I am grateful to T. O., who started it all.

In the face of all the guidance I have been given by those I've mentioned and others too numerous to list, any mistakes, omissions, or inaccuracies remain my responsibility alone.

Introduction

I am going to talk to you honestly about marijuana.
"Honestly" means that I will stick to the facts. Today we know a great
deal more about marijuana, and especially about how the brain is
prewired to respond to marijuana, than we did during the sixties, seventies, eighties, and even the early nineties. We are in the midst of an
exciting scientific revolution in our understanding of marijuana.
Unfortunately, the results of recent research findings have not yet
found their way into the public's awareness. Parents either struggle
with fears about their children smoking pot or wonder whether they
even need to be concerned, and many lack the facts to speak with
authority about the subject. Some parents used to smoke pot and others still do. Old myths about marijuana still cloud family discussions.
Marijuana: What's a Parent to Believe? is written to put the latest accurate information and realistic perspectives on marijuana in parents'
hands. It is committed to the belief that honest information is the best
tool available for protecting those we love the most. When we combine the facts with our values, we're equipped to create our own belief
system around marijuana and other drug use. At that point, we will
know what the best decisions are for our family and will no longer be
confused, uncertain, misguided, or blindly committed to old beliefs.

1

I am going to talk to you as parents.

Parents have a unique perspective on the world, born of their fierce love and responsibility for those who are still too young to protect themselves. Their profound commitment leads most parents to be willing to sacrifice many of their own interests to protect their children's health and safety. Cherished beliefs from childhood are reexamined, and changed, as they accept the responsibility for raising children. Many parents view marijuana, along with alcohol and all other drugs, from an angle different from that of their early years. Parents rightfully have one paramount concern—the health and safety (physically, emotionally, and spiritually) of their children. All thoughts about marijuana focus on how or whether this plant will enhance or jeopardize their children's future.

"Parents" are not restricted to those who brought a child into the world. Many other adults develop important emotional connections to a child, often very deep connections. Friends, relatives, teachers, baby-sitters, doctors, nurses, coaches, camp counselors, ministers, rabbis, police, and even crosswalk guards all contribute to the parenting every child receives. Anyone who has ever shared the responsibility and privilege of caring for children has stood in the role of parent. Anyone who has ever felt a stake in the future of a child, whether that child is his or her own, a neighbor's, or an excited kid standing in the line at the ice-cream store, has shared in the parenting of that child. And anyone who shares in that parenting needs to know at least as much about marijuana as the world is eventually going to teach children.

I am going to talk to you as a psychiatrist who has specialized in addiction medicine.

As a psychiatrist who has worked for more than twenty-five years with alcoholics and other drug addicts, I remain fascinated by the role

This

drugs play in altering our conscious experience, sometimes subtly, sometimes massively, and sometimes addictively. Marijuana has undergone several transitions within the course of my life. It began as an exotic, dangerous drug. Then it morphed into an agent of social change and became my friend. As more time passed, it became an enigma. Dangerous to some people, it seemed to remain relatively harmless entertainment to others. Gradually, marijuana's mystique has now given way to the disciplined probing of science. Research has completely shifted the focus away from marijuana itself. Just as Columbus set out to prove that the world is not flat and ended up discovering whole new continents, science set out to understand marijuana and ended up discovering unexplored portions of the brain. For an addiction psychiatrist, this is an extremely exciting and gratifying time. By helping to bring this story alive for readers, I hope to create a healthier perspective for talking to children about pot.

And I am going to talk to you as a parent myself.

I come to the topic of what parents need to know about marijuana from a very personal direction. The generation before me and the generation following me have fought their chemical demons. First it was my father's alcoholism that disrupted my family and then my child's marijuana dependence. I have personally experienced the whirlpool of dread and doubt that appears when a child begins to slip into addiction. I have felt crisis advance haltingly before it was suddenly upon me with a vengeance. And I know what it is like to be caught up in the swirl of anger, self-recrimination, and impotence that transforms a home into trench warfare. My escalating efforts to control someone else's addiction had the same impact as tossing gasoline on a raging fire. For a time, marijuana came to symbolize the crumbling of dreams for my family's, and my child's, future.

That was then. A lot has happened since recovery entered our home and freed each of us from the worst of our fears. I have also experienced the other side of the whirlpool of addiction—the side where everyone emerges stronger than ever, more deeply in touch with themselves, and connected to one another more than ever, and healthier than ever. Once again, my perspective on marijuana has changed.

Use of marijuana always entails risk. The risk to some people is quite a bit greater than to others. The two biggest risks come with youth and family history. The younger someone is when he or she first starts smoking marijuana, the greater risk that person runs of developing problems. And the greater the history of addiction in a person's extended family, the greater risk he or she runs when using marijuana, as is true with any other potentially addictive drug.

In marijuana's case, however, addiction may not be the greatest risk. Physical addiction to marijuana *does* exist, despite many claims to the contrary. Several lines of evidence all point to the reality of marijuana addiction. But the physical addiction is not as powerful as with many other drugs and does not influence everyone the same way. Marijuana can be a seductive drug for many people, especially for adolescents, who are in critical (and often difficult) stages of psychological development. Just at the stage when teenagers are most bored with their childhood ways and most interested in transcending the life they have known up to that point, marijuana provides an expressway to change that dead end up ahead, somewhere still out of sight. This is the risk youngsters expose themselves to when they experiment with marijuana. For a majority, the risk will be taken without significant consequences. For a minority, however, marijuana will derail development, sometimes with serious consequences for them and their families.

To understand the allure to many, and the risk to some, we must first understand the inside story. What is it about the human brain that causes us to react so strangely, so powerfully, and at times so disastrously to oily resins produced by the cannabis plant?

Chapter 1

Cannabis:
Putting Pot into Perspective

People have different experiences with alcohol and other drugs. Our relationship with them is not too different from the way we relate to cars, actually. Some people have no interest in driving and never learn; others are off racing just as soon as they can. Some take a few risks on the road, get away with their youthful foolishness without any serious consequences, and then settle down into safer driving habits. Others crash and burn before they have a chance to reach their adult years. Sometimes horrible outcomes seem nearly inevitable, given a child's personality. Other times life seems unreasonably arbitrary, as an otherwise cautious driver takes one needless risk and pays the ultimate price.

As parents, we have to stand by as our adolescents begin exercising choices that we have little opportunity to oversee and even less power to control. Statistics show that the first few years of driving are the most dangerous, and so we prepare our children as best we can. We teach them the rules and mechanics of driving but are powerless to ensure that they bring good judgment into their newfound freedom on a dark Saturday night. We are at the mercy of their independent decisions. The stakes are high, too high not to worry. The car is taking them away from the family, out into the world. We can no longer control their destination as they drive off on their own trajectories. We are left behind to hope, to have faith, and to pray until we hear the car's motor safely in the driveway again.

Alcohol and other drugs also have the power to take adolescents away from the family, out into the world. Unless we chain our children inside the house and prevent friends from visiting, we find ourselves at the mercy of their decisions about whether to drink or take other drugs. Some will have no interest and avoid taking any risks. Others will seek every opportunity to experience drugs with a hunger that can quickly consume them. Many in this latter group will take risks without suffering any obvious consequences, perhaps even learning useful lessons about themselves and their judgment. But others will experiment only a very few times and suffer severe and lifelong consequences.

The common denominator between driving and using drugs or drinking alcohol is that *use equals risk*. There is no way around this equation. Use the car and we put ourselves, and others, at risk. People generally feel that the benefit of driving is great enough, and that most teens are competent and responsible enough, to justify the risks inherent in driving. We do what we can to minimize those risks and then try to let go. It works out well enough for most of us. Another commonality between driving and drugs is that most people don't enter into use of either with the intention of meeting disaster. Most people don't speed along a dark and winding highway or drag race through city streets in order to crash and burn. In the same way, most people don't begin using drugs or drinking alcohol to become an addict. Sometimes adolescents' stupendous sense of invulnerability shields them from seeing the risks they are taking. Other times they are ignorant of the risks, and occasionally they simply do not care if harm comes. Whatever the reasons, to adolescents it often seems that trouble strikes suddenly—when the tires begin skidding off the road or when drug withdrawal has them in its grips.

In general, the risks in using mind-altering chemicals are greater and the benefit is more questionable than with driving. A much higher percentage of adolescents experience negative consequences from using chemicals, including marijuana, than from driving. In an effort to minimize these risks, we have in the United States made most drug use illegal for all ages and prohibited drinking before age twenty-one. In truth, we are far more effective in keeping underage drivers off the road than we are at keeping drug use and underage drinking from happening.

Despite legal efforts to prevent the use of drugs such as marijuana, alcohol, amphetamines, cocaine, heroin, and hallucinogens by adolescents (and adults, except for alcohol), the truth is that our children live in an open drug bazaar. They are surrounded by every opportunity imaginable, and those who are naturally curious will hear the opportunities knocking. It is a delusion to believe we can build a fence around our children to keep drugs and alcohol out of their lives. Therefore, we need to take off our blinders and do what we can to prepare them to make healthy choices when confronted with the availability of drugs and alcohol and to recognize as quickly as possible when they are making unhealthy decisions.

Marijuana: A Product of Cannabis

I have written this book to help parents help their children. The goal is for everyone to make good (that is, *healthy*) decisions, especially about marijuana—one of the three drugs children are most likely to encounter during their teen years; the other two are alcohol and tobacco. People make healthy decisions when they know the objective facts and combine that information with their values to create a belief system to guide them. Every parent, as well as every adolescent, benefits from knowing the basic facts about marijuana—what it is, how it works, the many ways it can affect adolescent development, its addictive and seductive potential—and how to recognize teens whose lives have begun to spin out of control because of it.

Marijuana comes from a weed, quite literally, which is why it is often called *weed* or *herb*. The common cannabis plant probably originated in Central Asia but grows nearly everywhere around the globe. Several varieties of hemp, as the plant is more commonly called, have been cultivated throughout the centuries for its valuable fiber, which supplied much of the rope used on early sailing ships.

The psychoactive properties produced by cannabis are primarily due to a molecule named tetrahydrocannabinol, or THC. THC is concentrated in the oily resin found in the leaves of both male and female plants and especially in the female flowers (which is why marijuana is also called *bud*). Underground horticulturists have created hybrids of *Cannabis sativa*, which reaches a height of fifteen feet under optimal conditions, and *Cannabis indica*, which is a smaller bush (four feet tall). Careful cross-fertilization has progressively increased the content of THC from 1 to 3 percent in the 1960s to more than 20 percent in some varieties found today. When the leaves and buds are dried and gathered together, the product becomes what we call "marijuana."

A Brief History: Pot as a Cultural and Political Symbol

Although hemp was grown in the United States during colonial times for industrial uses (rope, fabric, paper) and "tincture of cannabis" was used widely in the mid–nineteenth century to treat a variety of ills, the use of marijuana as a means of getting high did not begin in this country until the early 1900s. Immigrant farmworkers from Mexico, where marijuana was widely ingested by smoking it as cigarettes, first passed the idea (and the word "marijuana") on to African Americans in border towns and ports such as El Paso and New Orleans. The marijuana cigarettes, once called *muggles* in the South, eventually came to be called *joints*. (When cigars are emptied of tobacco and filled with pot, they may be called *blunts*.) Smoking remains the main way to use marijuana.

National awareness of marijuana developed, and was manipulated, in the early 1930s by Henry Anslinger, the first commissioner of the U.S. Bureau of Narcotics and former assistant commissioner of Prohibition. He campaigned vigorously against the drug by exaggerating its role in violent crime, which he often described in inflammatory racist terms. He set a hysterical tone for the government in his negative reactions to marijuana, as exemplified by the antipot movie *Reefer Madness* (1936) that is so closely associated with his name. As a result of the tone he set, most Americans were ill prepared to distinguish marijuana from heroin and amphetamines when in the 1960s its use moved out of the small world of beat poets and African American musicians into the hippie revolution within the heartland of white society.

What makes marijuana's history relevant to parents today is that most Americans, and many drug policy makers within the government, still view the drug from a perspective that arose out of the social turmoil that started escalating in the early sixties. Somehow, marijuana became the symbol par excellence for youthful rejection of authority and more. Much more. All traditional values seemed to be jettisoned by the act of lighting up a joint. The reaction to this "revolution" was a highly politicized, punitive, and often violent War on Drugs. Politicians zealously demonized marijuana as much as hippies blindly glorified the weed. The middle ground disappeared, objectivity became nearly impossible, and intelligent dialogue about marijuana was, and still remains, rare.

The same polarized perspectives that divided America in the sixties are alive in homes today. To many adolescents, pot still symbolizes freedom and self-will. To many parents, it symbolizes defiance and loss of control. An irony not lost on teens is that a significant number of today's parents at least experimented with pot during their youth, perhaps even in defiance of *their* parents, and that some parents still smoke pot.

Fortunately, scientific discoveries over the past decade provide us with valuable new ways of thinking about marijuana. Solid information about how and why THC affects the brain provides an escape from the polarized perspectives that have paralyzed rational dialogue about marijuana in America.

Is Marijuana Really a Problem Drug?

Before diving into what scientists have learned about marijuana, objective answers to two questions help put pot into perspective: (1) Just how widespread is marijuana use? (2) How much does pot actually contribute to America's total drug problem?

We have credible answers for the first question. Marijuana is by far the most frequently used illegal drug in America—not only by adolescents but by adults as well. In 1999, the National Household Survey on Drug Abuse conducted by the Substance Abuse and Mental Health Services Administration (SAMHSA) found that 76 million U.S. adults (approximately one-third of the adult population in the United States) reported having used marijuana at least once in their lives. About 9 percent had smoked pot in the previous year and 5 percent in the previous month. The age distribution of those who smoked pot during the previous month peaks at ages eighteen through nineteen, with over 17 percent reporting use. This monthly rate falls to 7.6 percent by age twenty-five.

Another survey, Monitoring the Future (http://monitoringthefuture.org), conducted by the University of Michigan, has closely followed drug use patterns in eighth and tenth graders since 1991 and in twelfth graders since 1975. The number of eighth graders reporting using marijuana *at least once* has doubled in the last ten years, from

10 percent to more than 20 percent in 2001. Similarly, tenth-grade use has risen from 23 percent to 40 percent in 2001. Seniors in high school are currently at 49 percent. Surprisingly, perhaps, 47 percent of seniors in 1975 reported having tried marijuana, although this figure has been as high as 60 percent (1979) and as low as 32.5 percent (1992). Figure 1 shows how the percentage of students who have smoked marijuana *during the previous year* has varied.

Figure 1: Trends in Marijuana Use

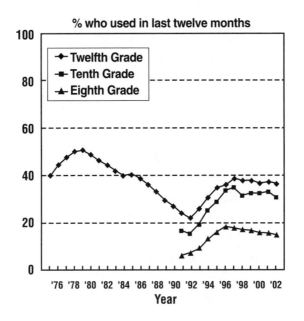

This figure illustrates the fluctuations in the percentage of high school seniors from 1976 to 2002 who used marijuana in the previous year. Eighth and tenth graders were surveyed beginning in 1991. (Courtesy of Monitoring the Future, Institute for Social Research, University of Michigan)

While eighth, tenth, and twelfth graders report rates of 20 percent, 40 percent, and 49 percent, respectively, for having smoked pot at least once (2001), the rates for having used during the previous month are 5.5 percent, nearly 9 percent, and nearly 11 percent, respectively. The rate of daily use among eighth graders is 1.3 percent; among tenth graders, 4.5 percent; and among twelfth graders, 5.8 percent. The only two drugs that more seniors have used are alcohol (80 percent) and tobacco (62 percent). The rates of other drug use by seniors are considerably lower than alcohol, tobacco, and marijuana; for example, amphetamines come in at 16 percent, hallucinogens (including Ecstasy) around 12 percent, cocaine at 8 percent, steroids under 4 percent, and heroin under 2 percent.

Clearly, a lot of people are smoking marijuana in the United States, although this does not distinguish us from most European countries, Canada, Australia, or New Zealand. Despite the government's efforts to reduce the supply of marijuana, an estimated 1.5 million youths between twelve and seventeen and about half a million young adults between eighteen and twenty-five used marijuana for the first time in 1999. This pervasive sea of cannabis tends to obscure an interesting fact that gets lost in the media and in most of our minds: *Nonusers outnumber users in every age category.* At no time in our child's life can it be claimed that "everyone is smoking pot," or even that "most people are smoking pot." The majority of kids, and the majority of adults, have never smoked pot.

Still, the extent of experimentation with marijuana is so great that nearly every child is bound to be exposed to opportunities to try it. Our sons and daughters will have to make very conscious decisions to avoid, or to delay, using marijuana. Often, the decision to abstain will be accompanied by discomfort and pain when they are excluded from groups or activities that they may want to join. At other times, youngsters who choose to abstain will be denying their own native curiosity about an experience that some of their peers are touting as "incredible, man!" Few are immune from having to make the tough decisions about which risks to take and which to avoid. And none are immune from having to take responsibility for the consequences of the decisions they make.

So, we do know how widespread marijuana use is, but the answer to our second question—How much does pot actually contribute to America's total drug problem?—is more difficult to nail down. Conventional wisdom within the chemical dependence field traditionally estimates that two-thirds of all problems (health, legal, and economic) caused by drugs and alcohol in the United States stem from alcohol alone. The remaining one-third of the damage is caused by all other drugs (except nicotine) put together. Tobacco is in a category all by itself, responsible for 430,000 deaths each year—more than all other drugs combined.[1] Alcohol contributes to 100,000 deaths annually. This number dwarfs the 9,484 deaths attributed to nonmedical use of all other drugs in 1996 (alcohol was also involved in 37 percent of these deaths).[2]

While nearly one out of every four hospital admissions is caused or complicated by alcohol, marijuana's contribution to disease and accidental trauma is several orders of magnitude less.[3] It is unclear whether any deaths have ever been directly attributable to marijuana overdose alone. Compared with other frequently used drugs, a small percentage of people eventually become dependent upon marijuana. An Institute of Medicine Report (1999) estimates that the dependence risk for any adult who has ever used tobacco is 32 percent, 23 percent for heroin, 17 percent for cocaine, 15 percent for alcohol, and 9 percent for cannabis.

Statistics clearly show that only a minority of adolescents who experiment with marijuana ever "go off the deep end" with it. But statistics are meaningless when we believe our own child has begun to fall into a destructive relationship with alcohol, marijuana, or any other drug. Who cares whether the majority of tenth graders have never experimented with pot when we see our child drawing away from nonusing friends to hang out more and more with kids whose main connection is that they get stoned together? What consolation is it that few, if any, people have died as a direct result of marijuana when we suspect that our ninth grader may also be smoking cigarettes, bingeing with alcohol, and riding around with a drunk driver? Some kids stick to marijuana alone, but many others soon branch out, piling risk on top of risk, multiplying the chances that the consequences will be severe. As long as no negative consequences have occurred yet, most adolescents see this as proof that no negative consequences *will* happen.

Marijuana's Special Role in Adolescence

Adolescent development is sometimes smooth, but more often there is some turmoil along the way. It is not simply the number of changes that adolescents have to integrate—puberty, new interest in sexuality, increased ability to comprehend the adult world, new freedom, and responsibility—that challenges them, but that these changes also happen at depths many teens previously had no awareness existed within them. An impulse to separate in new ways from parents, a longing to be intimate, a hunger for competence (not always accompanied by a willingness to work toward this goal), disillusionment in their parents that follows giving up childish views of how perfect they were—all these changes rumble deep within.

There are no easy remedies for the teen's turmoil. It is exciting, scary, confusing, and challenging all at once—often for both the teen and his or her parents. Parents do not seem to offer solid answers, and teens do not really want answers from them. Like kit foxes exploring away from the den or fledglings whose time has come to test their wings against the wind, adolescents switch over to an internal authority rather than rest too comfortably, or too exclusively, on the external guidance of a parent. This shift toward independence requires deep and pervasive change within the private reaches of a child's mind and heart. As parents we don't escape the turmoil, because we are called upon to keep growing as well. There is nearly as much parent development as there is adolescent development that needs to occur during a child's teen years. This is especially true with a first child. The path toward independence that our child is forging needs to be paralleled by a parental path, one that leaves behind the director's role we took with the toddler and grade-schooler and evolves into the consultant's role that our teen needs. As consultant, we are no longer number one to him or her. We can no longer impose our will on him or her in most affairs. In fact, it becomes mandatory that we pick our battles more wisely, intruding on our child's life primarily in issues of health and safety. And parent and child are very likely to have differences of opinion regarding what might threaten health and safety.

For example, how much risk is our sixteen-year-old taking if he or she experiments a handful of times with marijuana? There is no blanket answer to this question. Every person is an individual, so the degree of risk has to be evaluated on an individual basis. Some kids inherit a family history of alcohol and other drug addiction; their risk will be higher than that of peers whose families do not have a history of addiction. Some adolescents are risk averse and will approach any new situation with caution. They will run lower risk than their friends who are naturally thrill seekers. And those teens who have a strong streak of defiance motivating them to experiment with drugs may well be at higher risk than those who are just satisfying their natural curiosity. Each child brings his or her own profile of vulnerabilities and resiliencies into whatever relationship he or she has with pot, and these factors will determine the degree of risk each is running.

Children do not grow up in isolation, however. Their vulnerabilities and resources are also affected by their family's health. Research has consistently shown that extreme parental attitudes, whether pro or con, about drugs tend to lead to increased drug use by offspring. Moderate parental attitudes that neither condemn nor are overly permissive lead to the healthiest attitudes toward alcohol and other drugs in children. As parents, we have a duty to work toward the healthiest understanding of, and personal relationship to, psychoactive chemicals that we can possibly achieve. Our responsibility to our children is to achieve a sophisticated, thoughtful perspective, not the knee-jerk, fear-driven reaction to drugs that may leap up from our gut when we sense a threat to our kids.

Unfortunately, such moderation is often misunderstood to mean that parents should accept that smoking a little dope is a "normal" part of adolescence. I have had many discussions (read "arguments") with school counselors who give the message to teens and their parents that experimenting with marijuana is normal. I understand that the counselors are trying to calm parents' fears. Because most kids who experiment with marijuana never become dependent upon it or get knocked off their normal developmental tracks by the experience, it is clearly best that their parents not get hysterical. Overreactions can sometimes cause more of a problem than the experimentation itself.

But why should we accept the message that smoking pot is normal for adolescents when 51 percent—a majority—of high school graduates have never tried pot? Not smoking marijuana is at least as normal as some experimentation. In fact, I think we need to recognize that "normal" has a broad range. (If being a psychiatrist has taught me anything, it has taught me that there is a huge range of normal among humans.) I am content to say that many healthy kids experiment with marijuana *and* that many equally healthy kids choose not to. "Normal" includes both nonusers and infrequent users. As messy as this formulation is, it appears to be the reality. As parents, we muddle the situation if we impose our black-and-white thinking on children. Not all who use are in trouble, and not all use is trouble free. Everyone who uses places himself or herself at some risk. For a substantial minority, the negative consequences can range anywhere from temporary to devastating. As parents, we need to educate ourselves enough to recognize when simple experimentation has slid into abuse and when abuse has plummeted into dependence.

Our Own Relationship with Alcohol and Other Drugs

The job begins for parents with taking a hard, piercing look at our own relationship to alcohol and other drugs. It is literally impossible to take a healthy stance toward our children's behavior around drugs if we are not honest about our own relationship with drugs and alcohol. Every one of us has a relationship with alcohol and other drugs, whether we use them or not. If we drink, do we ever drink to excess? Do we ever drink more, or more often, than we consciously choose to? Do we drink to cope with life? Has drinking been integrated into the very fabric of our lives? Do the effects of alcohol substitute for functions our psychology should take care of (e.g., calming ourselves at the end of the day or preparing to socialize)? Do we mix up our right to drink with whether our health is being served well by how much we drink? Does alcohol ever distance us from our emotions and from other people? Why do we drink?

The same questions need to be faced if we use other drugs. Do we rely on prescription medications to deal with normal anxiety? Do we decide for ourselves when and how to use prescription painkillers? Are we willing to look realistically at both the benefits and the potential negative side effects of every drug we use? Are we addicted to cigarettes, and what message does this give? Do we bring illegal drugs into our house—marijuana, cocaine, amphetamines, opiates, hallucinogens, Ecstasy (even if only in small amounts)? Is there any drug use that we keep out of our children's sight (this is usually called "hiding")? Do we crawl under the porch on a Saturday afternoon so our twelve-year-old will not see us smoke a joint?

If we have any difficulty routinely facing daily life without modifying it a little, taking the "edge off," then we need to do the hard work of figuring out what makes our sober experience unacceptable. Unless we resolve this question, we can never approach our child with our integrity intact. Believe me, adolescents are great detectors and revealers of any lack of integrity. By being out of integrity, we lose the authority needed to teach the facts and our family's values about alcohol and other drugs. We will lose this authority because we are not living what we are teaching, and our words will be hollow. Adolescents hate hearing hollow words. They are quickly disillusioned by hypocrisy and react by pushing us away. It is only our integrity, honesty, and caring that will continue to attract our teenager into a meaningful relationship with us. This integrity includes looking with rigorous honesty at our own relationship to alcohol and other drugs.

If we do not use alcohol or other drugs, we still have to look deeply at the reasons for this choice. The values that motivate abstinence can range from health concerns to fear to moral rejection of the idea. I am not insisting that we explore our motivations for abstaining as a challenge but rather to see whether these feelings about drugs may be spilling over into feelings about *drug users*. If we disdain drug users because we see them as being inferior, weak, or sinful, we may be mixing up the effect of drugs on their lives with who the person using the drugs is underneath the behavior. If we fear the drug user because we fear the drug, we may be more likely to believe punitive approaches are needed to protect society and our family. If we condemn the drug on moral grounds, we may also unknowingly condemn the drug user. No amount of compassion can hide this undercurrent of moral rejection from drug users, addicts, and alcoholics. They will find an infinite number of ways to avoid being in meaningful conversation with any-one who disdains them.

It is not enough to look searchingly at our personal relationship with drugs. We must also take a hard look at our relationship to drug users, especially if we are a parent of a child whose life is being over-taken by drug use. We must find a way of being open to the person who is lost behind the behavior. Opening up to a drug user is extra-ordinarily difficult for many parents. We may be scared silly for our child's safety and disappointed by his or her behavior. We see the child callously stomping on our hopes for the future and can't com-prehend how our child could be so closed off to our concerns. Our dis-appointment often bleeds over into a wounded sense of pride: How could our child do this to us? "What is wrong with him?" becomes more of an accusation than a probing question.

How we feel about drug users will determine whether we are able to do our part in keeping an open dialogue with our children, avail-able whenever they wish to enter it. We can lead our children to the refreshing water of honest communication with us, and we can assure them that the water is clean, cool, and abundant, but we can never force them to drink it. As adolescents, they have the power to open their ears to us or not. Truly understanding this fact means accepting that we have become mere consultants. Perhaps we will be able to be the most important consultants in their lives, but we are consultants nonetheless.

Staying ahead of the Curve

Our job as parents with adolescents is often harder than when they were younger. We are no longer in control in the same way. We can no longer pick up the toddler who is about to run into the street and direct her back toward the playground. The fact that those days are over does not mean that we no longer have a job. It just means that our role has become a bit more difficult to conceptualize, and it is no longer as much at the center of our children's lives. We must let the center go, because a teen's core can no longer be grasped and held on to. We must accept our place more on the periphery of their lives. If we do not accept this with some grace, they will have to push harder to be rid of us. Their very maturation depends upon it.

One job that still remains as the parent of an adolescent is to stay ahead of the curve. We can predict the general outlines of what lies ahead of our teens better than they can, because they have never been this way before. We can predict that decisions about how they are going to relate to drugs and alcohol lie just ahead or may already surround them. If we are going to serve as a resource with any value to them in their decisions about marijuana, we need to learn more about the topic than they know. We need to have studied and thought about both the pros and the cons involved in issues swirling around marijuana. And, given recent astounding scientific discoveries, staying ahead of the curve also means gathering the most reliable information available about marijuana and how it affects the brain—why it works and why it doesn't.

If we sit back and permit our sons and daughters to rely on the information about pot bandied about by peers, we will fall too far behind the curve ever to be useful consultants for them. We need to take an active approach to understanding all the controversies about pot, including how these issues are being transformed by research, which has recently shown that our brains are prewired to respond to cannabis. Don't let the pot culture's myths and wishful thinking substitute for solid scientific information. Parents need to prepare themselves with hard information. With the facts. Whether a child is willing to hear what we have to say or not, the facts enable us to speak with calm authority—and that almost always eventually has an effect on a child, even if it's just planting a seed.

The Bottom Line

If our child is slipping away from us and losing control of his or her marijuana use, we are unlikely to recognize the truth about what is happening at the beginning. It takes time to put the pieces together. It takes time to take our blinders off. It takes time to deal with all the emotional reactions that are bound to arise once we do open our eyes. It will take even more time to communicate with our child's other parent, to come to agreement about what is happening and what to do. It usually also takes time for our response to the problem to influence our child. Throughout all this time, we still have the job of providing the necessities for our child's growth.

Providing basic needs means surrounding our child with a loving environment. We need to make a clear distinction between who our child is and what his or her behavior has become. Despite our fear and disappointment, we need to find a way to reject the behavior while accepting the child. This task, simple to describe, is often excruciatingly difficult, usually because the deeper the crisis becomes, the less our child accepts himself or herself. Our child's behavior may push us incessantly toward blaming, chastising, even hating him or her. Our job, if we are to help our teen grow out of self-imposed hell, is to maintain compassion for what lies underneath the misbehavior, while drawing clear boundaries around what is, and is not, acceptable.

Few of us parents can sustain this difficult task for long on our own. So part of our job may be to find the support we need in order to continue loving our troubled, and troubling, child. Together we can do things that we cannot do alone.

Finally, occasionally a parent's job is to safeguard the bottom line, our child's health and safety. In the end, a teen's life is more important than his or her temporary freedom.

Let's start with the job that we will all face with adolescents: staying ahead of the curve. The next chapter turns to the fascinating story that researchers have recently unlocked for us—the story of our brains, why marijuana makes us high, and how it lets us down afterward.

Chapter 2

Marijuana and the Brain: Prewired for Pot

What happens when someone lights up a joint and pulls the smoke deeply into his or her lungs? What does getting "high" really mean, and how do chemicals that appear to be found uniquely in cannabis plants produce this feeling? In short, how does marijuana work?

Some Basic Brain Science

First, a general word about nerve communication: Each nerve is a single living cell. See figure 2 on page 24.

Communication between two nerve cells occurs chemically. Whenever a nerve cell "fires," the main body of the nerve sends a minute electrical disturbance rippling down its one long extension (the axon). What we normally think of as a nerve is actually a bundle of these threadlike extensions from individual nerve cells. (Scientists use the word *neuron* to refer to a single nerve cell to avoid confusion with the "nerves" that wire the brain to the rest of the body.) When an electrical impulse reaches the rootlike branching at the end of an axon, it causes a few tiny packets of a chemical, a neurotransmitter, to burst out of the cell. See figure 3 on page 24.

Figure 2: The Nerve Cell

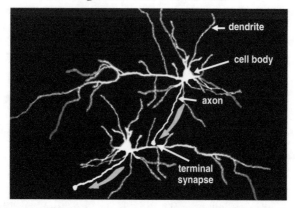

A view of two nerve cells through a microscope. Each cell consists of a cell body with multiple branches (dendrites) reaching out to sense the immediate environment. One long process (the axon) reaches out to contact the dendrites of other nerve cells. Communication between the two nerves happens when a small electrical impulse races along the axon away from the cell body. When the electrical impulse reaches the terminal synapse, it causes a neurotransmitter chemical to be released. (Adapted from an image from the National Institute on Drug Abuse, National Institutes of Health)

Figure 3: The Synapse

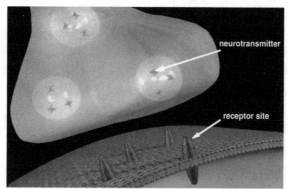

Nerve cells communicate by passing a neurotransmitter chemical from the end of one cell's axon to receptor sites on the dendrite of the next nerve cell. This activity takes place in an area of close connection called the synapse. (Adapted from an image from the National Institute on Drug Abuse, National Institutes of Health)

Although more than forty different neurotransmitters have been identified in the brain, each nerve cell appears to produce and use only one kind. The names of some of these neurotransmitters are becoming familiar to the general public, such as dopamine, serotonin, and endorphins. Others, such as GABA, norepinephrine, acetylcholine, and anandamide, are far less familiar. One important perspective to remember is that all neurons can be classified by the particular neurotransmitter they use. As a result, we can speak of the *system* of serotonin neurons, or dopamine neurons, and so on, within the brain. This is valuable background information for understanding both how marijuana affects the brain and the fundamental process of addiction.

What happens to neurotransmitter molecules once they are released from the end of a neuron's axon? Within five to seven thousandths of a second, most of the transmitter is vacuumed back up into the neuron to be repackaged and used again, while some is destroyed by enzymes outside the neuron before it can be recycled. During the brief time neurotransmitters remain outside the nerve cell, an astounding thing happens. Many of the neurotransmitter molecules briefly "stick" to the surface of the next nerve downstream. The sticking point, called a receptor site, is actually a small protein built into a nerve cell's outer membrane. These receptor sites are highly specific, acting like locks that can be entered and activated only by the right key. A neurotransmitter permits one nerve to communicate with the next by entering a receptor site for which it is uniquely designed. When a receptor site is activated, it either stimulates or suppresses activity of the nerve cell it is a part of. See figure 4 on page 26.

While this whole mechanism of neurotransmitters, receptor sites, and chemical communication might sound exotic at first, it is really no more mysterious than our sense of smell. If our eyes are closed when an orange is freshly cut, some of the fragrant molecules soon land on the nerves in our nose and we are able to identify the fruit immediately. If a lemon is cut, we quickly recognize its more sour odor. In a similar way, nerve cells communicate with each other largely through "smelling" each other's "fragrances."

Figure 4: Neurotransmitter Release and Receptor Site Activation

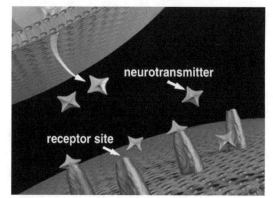

Neurotransmitters are released when an electrical impulse reaches the synapse at the end of a cell's axon. Neurotransmitters affect the next cell by fitting into specific receptor sites, likes keys into a lock. When a receptor site is activated by a neurotransmitter, it either stimulates or suppresses the cell that contains it. (Adapted from an image from the National Institute on Drug Abuse, National Institutes of Health)

Psychoactive chemicals affect neurons in two ways. The blunter approach is taken by alcohol, which generally poisons a neuron until it is no longer capable of firing. Alcohol incapacitates neurons and puts them to sleep. The second, more targeted way to affect neurons is to interact with their neurotransmitters and receptor sites. Some drugs imitate natural neurotransmitters; for example, heroin imitates endorphins, thereby stimulating neurons that contain endorphin receptor sites. Some drugs block neurotransmitters by occupying receptor sites without unlocking their activity. Some drugs cause more neurotransmitter molecules to be released each time a neuron fires. And some drugs interfere with the reuptake of neurotransmitters, thus prolonging their action; for example, Prozac slows down the recycling of serotonin.

When drugs work by interacting directly with neurotransmitters, a far smaller quantity needs to be ingested to have an effect. This is why no one has to drink four glasses of cocaine (which increases dopamine and norepinephrine activity) in order to get high, and no one can get drunk on alcohol by snorting a few drops up their nose. Most psychoactive drugs work in small quantities because they directly affect neurotransmitters. Until recently, however, no one understood how the THC in marijuana affected our brains. No one was able to identify that THC poisoned nerve cells in any blunt way, nor were they able to link THC to any direct effect on a neurotransmitter system. With the latest scientific discoveries, all that has changed.

THC, a Molecular Masquerader

The most astounding new discovery made by scientists during the 1990s is that cannabis-like molecules are an important part of the normal chemical balance within our brains. We all have a system of nerve cells that produce naturally occurring cannabinoid neurotransmitters that closely resemble the THC found in marijuana. Because THC mimics these normal cannabinoid neurotransmitters, our brains are essentially prewired to respond to the chemicals found in pot. Healthy brains depend on maintaining a delicate balance among many complex chemicals, just as any healthy ecosystem needs balance among all its parts. Smoking pot introduces a chemical intruder—a molecular masquerader—that pushes the brain far out of its normal balance. By understanding how smoking marijuana affects different parts of the brain, we can understand better why the drug produces its unique "high" and why this is so appealing to many people. This information also enables us to speak to adolescents from a place of greater authority, with knowledge that few of today's teens possess about the herb they are using.

The following is what happens when someone lights up a joint.

Heat from the burning leaves and flowers easily vaporizes some of the plant's oily resin, including psychoactive THC, or delta9-tetrahydrocannabinol, molecules. THC molecules are the most important ingredient in the pot's cloud of smoke and vapor because they are responsible for virtually all of marijuana's mind-altering power. Along with all the smoke and ashes of the burning pot, the cloud of THC molecules is sucked deeply into the lungs and held there as long as possible, where it is easily absorbed into the blood. Within seconds, the THC-rich blood goes to the heart and then immediately shoots up to the brain. By the time a joint is finished, the THC has already reached peak blood levels. Experienced marijuana smokers, using today's potent strains of grass, can often feel the effect of their first drag on a joint within seconds. Marijuana is smoked more often than eaten (in cookies or brownies) because inhalation produces almost immediate effects and allows more control over the amount being consumed and thus over how high one becomes.

To study the distribution of THC once it gets to the brain, scientists attached a radioactive marker to THC molecules that enabled them to be photographed. They discovered that, initially, the stream of THC carried by the blood spreads evenly throughout the brain. Wherever blood flows, so go the molecular gate-crashers. But surprisingly, the THC molecules quickly come to rest in specific areas of the brain. Individual molecules initially pass unheeded through the brain but then suddenly stick to the outer membrane of specific nerve cells. It was soon discovered that THC fits perfectly into receptor sites that had hitherto never been detected. In studying the way marijuana affects the brain, researchers were discovering a whole new neurotransmitter system.

An Earlier Story: The Endorphin System

At first, one might wonder why our brains would produce receptor sites for a chemical found in marijuana. Surely evolution has not conspired to provide us with a brain receptor that hangs around in anticipation of being flooded by a torrent of pot smoke someday. What sense would that make? It wouldn't make sense, but as soon as scientists photographed the distribution of THC throughout the brain, locked into naturally occurring *cannabinoid receptors*, they recognized that they had seen a similar story once before with endorphins.

Endorphins are the brain's natural painkillers and pleasure producers. They were discovered as a result of asking why the sticky stuff oozing out of poppies, which is used to make opium, heroin, and morphine, has such a powerful effect on our minds. First, scientists isolated opiate molecules from the poppy, labeled them with a radioactive marker, and then found that they attach to specific receptor sites already present in the brain. (For comparison purposes, there are only one-tenth as many opiate receptors as there are cannabinoid receptors.) Then researchers identified morphinelike chemicals naturally occurring within the brain that normally occupy these opiate receptors. Because the word *endogenous* means that these natural morphinelike molecules are formed within the brain (as opposed to *exogenous* opiates, which are ingested from the outside), the term *endorphin* was coined from the words *endogenous* and *morphinelike*. Opiates such as heroin and morphine affect our brains so powerfully and produce such good pain relief and euphoria (in higher doses) because they mimic our natural endorphins and flood opiate receptors with excess stimulation.

With this brief background, we are now ready to meet the brain's endogenous cannabinoid system—the *endocannabinoids*—molecules naturally occurring in the brain that are "THC-like."

The Endocannabinoid System

If we return to the stream of THC molecules headed to the brain after smoking pot, we would find that they do not encounter vacant receptor sites waiting idly for their arrival. A natural chemical, an endogenous cannabinoid, or endocannabinoid, that is not found in marijuana already occupies many of these sites. The THC bumps up against similar, cannabis-like molecules that scientists have discovered are normal compounds produced by the brain. These compounds are the keys used by some nerve cells to fit into the brain's cannabinoid receptor site locks. In 1992, Ralph Mechoulam, who had discovered the structure of THC thirty years earlier, first reported the structure of this endogenous cannabinoid, which he named *anandamide*. Since then, additional endogenous cannabinoids have been identified, and there may be more to come. When THC molecules arrive at receptor sites designed to interact normally with anandamide, they act on the brain by *mimicking* this natural brain chemical. THC mimics anandamide and then muscles it off the receptors because it has up to four times the affinity, or sticking power, for these receptors. THC also stimulates receptor sites more strongly than the brain's own anandamide does.

Once scientists discovered anandamide and its associated receptor sites, they began finding it nearly everywhere. All mammals, leeches, clams, and even the very primitive hydra contain anandamide within their nervous systems. Within the human brain, endocannabinoids are hardly an exotic, backwater chemical transmitter. In fact, most of the brain is influenced by this newly discovered neurotransmitter. In a personal correspondence, Mechoulam wrote, "There is barely a physiological system in which endocannabinoids are not involved. Hence its importance is far beyond that of THC and marijuana." We will look at the important mental functions of the brain's endocannabinoid systems later in this chapter.

So pot works by flooding parts of the brain that normally use anandamide with the great mimic THC, profoundly and unnaturally overstimulating endogenous cannabinoid neurons. Understanding the effects of THC thus becomes a question of better understanding the role of anandamide and what happens when its normal levels are thrown out of balance. Although anandamide is found throughout the brain, it is especially concentrated in the same specific areas in all mammals.

Figure 5: Localization of Cannabinoid Receptor Sites

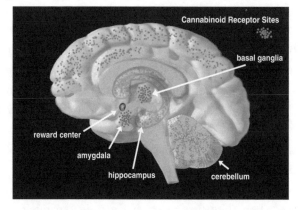

The THC in marijuana acts on portions of the brain that contain high concentrations of receptor sites for the brain's natural cannabinoid neurotransmitter anandamide. The areas most affected by THC include the hippocampus, amygdala, basal ganglia, cerebellum, and reward center. Receptor sites can also be seen throughout the cerebral cortex (the layer of nerves covering the surface of the brain), especially in the frontal lobes where the highest conceptual abilities and judgment reside. (Adapted from an image from the National Institute on Drug Abuse, National Institutes of Health)

Understanding the function of these endocannabinoid-rich areas can help explain the "high" that comes from smoking marijuana. And because every chemical action imposed on the brain is eventually followed by an equal and opposite reaction, understanding the parts of our brain that THC overstimulates also helps to explain the "low" that inevitably follows pot smoking.

The Hippocampus

One important destination for the THC is the hippocampus (the Latin name for seahorse, which this brain structure resembles), where endocannabinoid receptors are very dense. The hippocampus plays a critical role in short-term memory, boosting events in our immediate awareness into long-term memories. Most likely, anyone who has gotten high from marijuana has experienced its characteristic memory disruption, such as forgetting the beginning of a sentence before getting to the end. Conversations tend to get disjointed, veering off in unexpected directions. Tests in which people intoxicated with marijuana are asked to repeat increasingly long strings of random numbers, forward and backward, consistently show short-term memory impairment.

Fascinating results from animal studies have thrown light on the role of cannabinoids in the hippocampus. For example, two rats or two mice go through a stereotypical routine of sniffing about each other's face when they first meet. If they are separated and then reunited in less than two hours, they recognize each other enough to forgo this routine. However, if more than two hours pass, they have to get reacquainted all over by going through the whole sniffing process again. Under the influence of THC, however, the animals are not able to hold on to their memory of each other nearly as well. Their hippocampus shuts down a bit when overstimulated by the flood of THC, and they forget each other in less than an hour.

Intriguing clues to the normal function of anandamide and the other endocannabinoids in the hippocampus have begun to surface. For example, a chemical, SR141716A, has been developed that does the opposite of THC. Rather than stimulating endocannabinoid receptors, SR141716A occupies these receptors without activating them. SR141716A is a THC blocker—a cannabinoid antagonist. Studies on elderly rats reveal that blocking normal endocannabinoid activity actually prolongs their memory of each other. Apparently our cannabinoid system is designed to *modulate* the amount of short-term memory we have. Too little short-term memory and we can't finish our sentences coherently. Too much short-term memory and we probably couldn't learn anything new. It would be like trying to teach a class using a blackboard filled with last hour's notes and not having an eraser to clear the board for more information. A balanced, healthy endocannabinoid system is essential for efficient learning and memory.

The Amygdala

While some THC molecules land in the hippocampus, many others can be followed into an area of the brain called the amygdala (meaning "almond," which it resembles in size and shape), where they lock into an abundance of endocannabinoid receptors. Unlike the hippocampus, the amygdala has several functions, most of which are involved with assigning emotional relevance to our experience. More than any other part of our brain, perhaps, the amygdala lifts us above being mere robots. It is central to our emotional connectedness with each other and the bonding, suckling process that is unique to mammals. The amygdala is constantly monitoring our experience, giving a feeling of familiarity to whatever is repetitive, while imbuing novel events with the power to suddenly awaken our interest and capture our attention. A large proportion of the marijuana "high" is created by the impact of THC on the amygdala.

I think of the artificial stimulation of novelty created by THC as *virtual novelty*. By manipulating the chemistry that underlies our experience of novelty, marijuana turns the mundane into a source of artificial fascination. We become dis-habituated to parts of our experience that we have come to ignore because of its pervasive presence. A person stoned on pot suddenly notices the little rainbow gracing the curve of every single soap bubble in the dishwater. The senses feel "turned on"—enhanced by a renewed sensitivity. Movies are seen for the fourth time with "fresh" eyes, as though never truly seen before. Tastes blast out of the commonplace that they have fallen into through overfamiliarity. Herein lies much of the seduction of marijuana, both for adolescents and adults, and much of the pleasure.

Although people commonly report that their senses have become more acute, laboratory tests confirm that our sensitivity to sounds and color is actually unchanged by marijuana. When measured objectively, people are not able to hear softer sounds or to make subtler color distinctions when stoned. It is only our reactions to what we hear and see that is changed by marijuana. Still, many people are deeply fascinated by their different experience of the world when high. As the virtual novelty created by THC focuses their attention on details normally overlooked, they come to rediscover some of the richness that is necessarily lost when our brains habituate to common experiences.

Two additional functions of the amygdala stimulated by THC contribute to the pull a marijuana high exerts on many people. First, a small area within the amygdala produces a global sense of awe and ineffability when stimulated. This pleasant experience was first discovered when neurosurgeons used small electrodes in the amygdala during surgical procedures on humans who were alert and awake (brain tissue itself has no pain sensation). People described an almost spiritual sense of awe simply as a result of low currents of electricity activating areas that we now know to contain high concentrations of anandamide. This may explain the "Wow!" reaction that people high on marijuana often have when confronted with anything rich and complex.

A second fascinating function of the amygdala stems from its role in early suckling. Because mammals feed their young at the breast, it is essential that newborns have a strong impulse to suckle. When scientists administered the cannabinoid blocker SR141716A to rat pups within the first twenty-four hours of life, the pups essentially turned off all naturally occurring cannabinoid activity. As a result, the pups failed to suckle and eventually died. Apparently one function of our brain's endocannabinoid system is to promote the suckling and bonding critical to a mammal's early survival. These intertwined processes, one emotional and the other physiological, may well underlie the enjoyable "munchies" that attack many people who are stoned. Suddenly there is a nearly overwhelming desire for a wide variety of comfort foods, from brownies to Brie. The munchies do not result from the mere stimulation of naked appetite but are also an emotional experience.

The Loss of Valuable Receptor Sites

The flooding of endocannabinoid receptors by THC is not the end of the story. The brain is an ecosystem, and like a meadow or forest, it immediately responds to any disturbance by trying to undo an impact imposed from the outside. For every action there is an equal and opposite reaction. Soon after THC lands on receptor sites, whether in the hippocampus, the amygdala, or other parts of the brain, the number of sites begins to dwindle. At first, the overstimulation causes nerves to start sucking receptor sites into the cell, where they are no longer available to be stimulated. If the THC's unnatural storm continues, this down-regulation gradually leads to the actual dismantling of sites, which takes longer to reverse once the THC stimulation stops. As a result of the down-regulation of receptor density, when the high wears off and THC levels fall, the entire cannabinoid system enters into a state of endocannabinoid deficiency. Until the brain can rebuild receptors, anandamide and other endocannabinoids no longer have as many locks to key into. The system has been "dumbed down." Recovery time—the time it takes for the brain to rebuild endocannabinoid receptor sites—depends on how long the overstimulation has lasted and can take days, weeks, or even months. During this period of cannabinoid deficiency, a person can be motivated to smoke marijuana again in order to temporarily experience more "normal" brain levels of cannabinoid activity.

Imagine now, the next morning, when the teacher presents a novel idea in algebra class or describes a new concept in social studies. After having been overstimulated by THC, the amygdala now has fewer cannabinoid receptor sites. It will take more than the usual amount of novelty for the amygdala to recognize that something new is happening. The novelty experience generator is tired. The capacity to receive this new information with a full experience of its novelty is reduced because the endocannabinoid system is out of balance while the nerves are still in the process of rebuilding receptor sites. Natural interest is not peaked. The smoker thinks, *School is boring. Nothing interesting ever happens here. I can't wait to get out of class and smoke a joint.* Or imagine the athlete who is confronted the day after being high by an opponent who throws a new move in the game. Because the amygdala is sluggish, in the aftermath of having been overstimulated the night before, the novelty of the move does not register right away. Half a step is gained by the other side. And half a step may be all that is needed to be beaten. The aftereffects of pot are the loss of edge, the diminishing of optimal performance. Only after the system returns to its normal balance, or is again stimulated by the THC in marijuana, will interest and novelty reawaken fully, even if it is in the same mundane things that entertained the adolescent yesterday.

The decrease in the number of receptor sites after exposure to THC is real. Scientists have observed this reality in animals after even short exposures to THC. The behavioral effect of this decrease in receptors is also measurable. For example, commercial airline pilots were tested in flight simulators twenty-four hours after smoking a joint. Their performance on overlearned, routine takeoffs and landings showed no impairment. As soon as unexpected events were thrown into the mix, however, the pilots showed a reduced ability to respond quickly and effectively, as compared with their own normal performance. The pot caused difficulties by diminishing the pilots' capacity to notice and respond to novelty. With chronic, heavy pot use, this reduced capacity to experience novelty can produce such profound apathy in adolescents that the process of maturation stalls.

The Cerebellum and Basal Ganglia

THC molecules that do not attach to receptor sites in the hippocampus or amygdala may land in two areas important to our motor system—the cerebellum and the basal ganglia, each containing high levels of endocannabinoids. The basal ganglia begin the translation of "images of achievement" formulated by the highest portions of the brain into the actions and movements needed to achieve our goal. In other words, the basal ganglia turn our intention to catch a towering fly ball headed toward center field into all the instructions our arms and legs need to start running and to make the catch. The cerebellum works out the fine details. Like a computer, it constantly calculates the exact angles to take, the speed needed, and the timing of when to raise our glove to snatch the ball out of the air. We could never accomplish all this if we had to consciously direct every muscle group. The endocannabinoid-rich motor areas of the brain help accomplish this for us.

Flooding these motor areas with THC produces a variety of effects. Spontaneous activity is clearly diminished, which can undoubtedly have a calming effect (especially for people with attention deficit hyperactivity disorder). Animals become almost motionless (not paralyzed, because they can move if prodded sufficiently) with high doses of THC. Fine motor control is impaired; we become slightly clumsy when stoned. Tests of driving skills reveal that people try to compensate for their motor impairments by slowing down and being more careful. These compensations are undoubtedly complicated by the distortions of time and space perception that are part of being high, when time goes slower and distances seem larger. This is very different from people intoxicated with alcohol, who tend to overestimate their skill and actually speed up, a dangerous combination for drivers.

Despite an objective decline in motor control, many people paradoxically report very pleasant physical experiences when stoned, especially when dancing or performing repetitive behaviors (such as running or preparing foods). The experience can be one of greater flow. Like the runner's high, flow is a state of little or no resistance. One motion seems to glide effortlessly into the next. Perhaps the increased cannabinoid activity in motor areas provided by THC "greases" the translation of an impulse to move into practical instructions to the body. When the flow of dancing is combined with the altered perception of music caused by the amygdala's creation of virtual novelty, the experience can become all-encompassing.

Again, while overstimulation is occurring, the number of receptor sites for endocannabinoids in the motor areas immediately begins diminishing. First the sites sink below the surface and then they begin to be dismantled. The result is a state of anandamide and other endocannabinoid deficiency—the "burned out" aftermath of smoking pot—once the THC has worn off.

The Nucleus Accumbens, the Reward Center

There is another important place where high concentrations of THC attach to receptor sites normally occupied by endocannabinoids—a group of nerve cells that scientists have at different times called the pleasure center, the reward center, or just the nucleus accumbens. Following activities that normally give us pleasure, such as a good meal or sexual activity, levels of the neurotransmitter dopamine rise in the nucleus accumbens. All drugs capable of producing addiction appear to stimulate high—often unnaturally high—levels of dopamine in this nucleus. As a result, this small clump of cells is now seen as playing a critical role in addiction to alcohol and all other drugs of abuse.

When THC enters this small brain structure and performs its mimicry of the brain's normal endocannabinoids, it produces precisely the same changes as alcohol, nicotine, heroin, or cocaine. Pot also increases the level of dopamine in the reward center. The importance of this effect is so great that the following chapter is devoted to the question of marijuana's addictive potential.

The Bigger Picture

The hippocampus, the amygdala, the cerebellum and basal ganglia, and the nucleus accumbens stand out as important destinations for THC. But the stream of molecules supplied by marijuana finds receptor sites throughout the brain—including the whole cortex, especially the frontal lobes, where our highest abilities to think abstractly reside; the hypothalamus, where many of our appetites are regulated; olfactory areas; and even the pituitary, which regulates much of our endocrine system. Throughout all these areas, it appears that the role of our endocannabinoid system is to regulate the activity of the brain's other neurotransmitters. For example, close examination of microanatomy in the hippocampus reveals that endocannabinoid receptor sites often lie right at the tips of neurons that use GABA as a neurotransmitter. Increasing or decreasing the amount of cannabinoid activity in turn increases or decreases the amount of GABA that is released whenever its nerve fires. The endocannabinoid neurons appear to work by modulating the level of GABA activity. Wherever the endocannabinoid system is investigated, it always seems to work primarily by modulating the activity of other neurotransmitter systems.

While it would probably not be accurate to call endocannabinoids the "master regulators" of our brain's chemistry, a term like that would begin to get across how essential the work of anandamide and similar endocannabinoids are in adjusting the sensitivity of individual nerve cells to the whole host of chemical influences being brought to bear on them. Therefore, whenever the endocannabinoid system is out of balance, as it is when subjected to marijuana, the balance of multiple other systems in the brain is also disrupted.

Earlier in history, explorers searching for a Northwest Passage to the Orient ended up discovering a whole new continent. In a similar vein, neuroscientists searching for an understanding of how marijuana produces its high have discovered an important and widespread portion of the brain heretofore never seen—the "endocannabinoid continent." We are just in the earliest stages of exploring this vast new discovery. It is an exciting time for modern-day explorers.

The Aftermath

As I said earlier, for every chemical action we impose on the brain there is eventually an equal and opposite reaction. The calming effect of alcohol is followed the next day by the jangle and irritation of a hangover. The artificially high energy from caffeine, cocaine, and amphetamine is followed by a slump into lethargy. The pain-free haze of heroin is followed by acute sensitivity to every discomfort. Marijuana is no different. Although the aftermath of getting high is subtle, it can be cumulative. Relaxation can be followed by irritability. Fascination can be followed by boredom. Sensory enhancement can be followed by feeling flat. Awe can be followed by spiritual depletion. The emotional sense of relevance and connectedness can be followed by alienation. The decrease in short-term memory does not appear to be followed by an increase in memory, however, but rather by a lingering lack of clarity that active smokers rarely notice. Like a fog that develops so slowly that its growth cannot be noticed from day to day, marijuana can slowly cloud a person's view of the real world.

In sum, smoking pot profoundly alters brain chemistry, inducing the "high" that leads to a cumulative impairment of the important endocannabinoid system by decreasing critical receptor sites. The loss of clarity it creates is not only intellectual but emotional and spiritual as well. Unless they are actively smoking, chronic pot smokers tend to be bored and apathetic. Chronic pot smokers who are adolescents become increasingly ineffective in recognizing and meeting the normal challenges of psychological development. Their willingness to make an effort to reconnect with the world decreases as they develop the habit of using marijuana to reignite a sense of engagement in their lives. For the pot smoker, relief is only a puff away.

Does turning repeatedly to marijuana to dissipate boredom ever rise beyond seduction to the level of being a true addiction? The next chapter explores the different lines of reasoning regarding whether marijuana is addictive.

Chapter 3

Marijuana Addiction?
What Is the Evidence?

Is addiction too strong a word to apply to marijuana? We don't see marijuana junkies passed out in the gutter. We don't see marijuana addicts shaking and sweating or vomiting and hallucinating from withdrawal. We've never had to rush anyone to the emergency room in a coma from a pot overdose or witnessed anyone crashed in bed for forty-eight hours after bingeing uncontrollably on marijuana alone. Can marijuana be placed in the same addictive category as alcohol, heroin, cocaine, and amphetamines?

The Nature of Addiction
The medical field doesn't usually use the word *addiction*. Instead, physicians and psychologists think in terms of *use*, *abuse*, and *dependence*. These three terms offer a more flexible way of looking at an individual's relationship with alcohol and other drugs than does the more black-and-white question of whether someone is addicted.

Use
Marijuana *use* can be either purely experimental or a more ongoing recreational relationship. In either case, the hallmark of any drug use is that it is not causing psychological or family problems, failure to fulfill responsibilities (financial, school, or work), or creating undue

physical risk. In other words, *use* is *nonproblematic*. When use is truly experimental, it is rarely repeated more than a few times. When it becomes recurrent, especially when it threads through many social interactions with peers, the drug use has become an ongoing recreational activity. Because so many adolescents do have either an experimental or a recreational relationship with pot (in the 2001 Monitoring the Future survey, 49 percent of seniors had tried marijuana at least once and 11 percent had smoked within the past month), many adults oppose automatically labeling marijuana users as troubled kids.

Abuse

Marijuana *use* can slip imperceptibly into *abuse*, although this is far from an inevitable progression. Abuse heralds a maladaptive pattern of use, a harmful involvement with pot. Concrete problems have begun to appear, such as a decline in grades, school suspensions, increased family arguments, loss of interest in typical activities, driving while high, legal entanglements, or loss of friends. It is not always easy to determine when use has slid into abuse. Different people, including different professionals, draw the invisible line between use and abuse differently. Sometimes the onset of problems is not clearly connected to marijuana use (*"I failed the test because I'm not interested in math anymore"*), and believable rationalizations often obscure the onset of abuse. One parent may recognize that the developmental task of establishing a strong sense of identity is being interfered with by his or her teen's adopting the values of a stoner crowd, while another parent may excuse this as "just a phase; kids will be kids." The more informed we are about the effects of marijuana, the more quickly we may see negative consequences from its use; while the more denial we are in, the longer we will take to see a particular pattern of marijuana use as abuse. As parents, we are called upon to compare notes with as many other parents as possible to understand the limits of normal adolescent behavior but ultimately to trust our own instincts with our own children.

Dependence

Marijuana abuse can slide back to use or can persist for years. It can also advance to marijuana *dependence*, which is an extension of *abuse*, containing new definable and recognizable behaviors. The current standard used by physicians and psychologists for defining dependence on any psychoactive chemical is published by the American Psychiatric Association in DSM-IV (the *Diagnostic and Statistical Manual of Mental Disorders*). DSM is an ongoing effort to improve the objective criteria used for identifying any psychiatric condition. A work that is always in progress, it is currently in its fourth edition and is being actively revised as research provides more data. Insurance companies rely upon DSM to clarify the conditions for which they will authorize reimbursement to therapists.

Traditionally *tolerance* and *withdrawal* have always been included as physical evidence of dependence. Tolerance means that a person's body has gotten used to the presence of a drug and requires larger quantities to produce a high. Tolerance with alcohol, heroin, cocaine, and prescription painkillers is marked and clear. Many people experience less effect with frequent use of these drugs and begin escalating the amount they must consume to get high, often doubling or tripling their initial dose within a few weeks or months. Tolerance is less clear with marijuana. Some of the physical reactions to THC, such as rise in heart rate and lowering of pressure within the eyes, soon lessen unless the amount being smoked is increased. But most people do not use pot to experience these physical changes and so are unaware of the development of tolerance in these ways. On the other hand, many people report that they get high more easily after they learn how to use pot. Once they know what experiences to look for when smoking marijuana, they notice that the mental changes occur more quickly. Although this "reverse tolerance" has often been held to be unique by marijuana smokers, I have had several alcohol drinkers report the same phenomenon once they began trying to notice the earliest effects of drinking. Marijuana smokers who become dependent are less likely to begin consuming larger and larger amounts each time they smoke but rather to begin smoking more frequently throughout the day, until they are continuously high.

Withdrawal means that the body has come to expect the presence of a drug and goes through an uncomfortable readjustment to its absence. Physical withdrawal means that the brain has been so modified by the presence of the drug that it now depends upon that presence to operate as normally as possible. Once the drug is "withdrawn," the brain must undo the changes wrought by the drug to regain its normal baseline chemical balance. While the brain is busy correcting itself, the individual suffers symptoms unique to the drug being withdrawn. Again, alcohol, heroin, and cocaine withdrawal is dramatic and virtually impossible to hide. While physical withdrawal from marijuana does exist, it is often so muted that it is missed or attributed to other causes (*"You'd be irritable, too, if someone were bugging you all weekend to do stupid chores"*). More about marijuana withdrawal in a moment.

Drug *dependence* can exist, however, even in the absence of physical tolerance and withdrawal. The DSM lists other behaviors that are often referred to as signs of psychological dependence. These behavioral criteria defining dependence include loss of control of how much or how often marijuana is smoked, unsuccessful efforts to quit or cut down use, the devotion of great effort and time to finding and using pot (or to recovering from its effects), and abandoning social, academic, and recreational activities in favor of smoking. The final criterion, *continued use of marijuana despite recurrent adverse consequences*, is perhaps the clearest indication of psychological dependence. Such continued use in the face of problems created by smoking marijuana usually involves *disordered thinking*, most notably blatant *denial* of the obvious.

Chemical dependence is a complex disease that goes well beyond the stereotyped images many people have. Any three of the preceding criteria have to be present within the same twelve-month period to make a diagnosis in adults of dependence on any drug. We don't have to be falling-down drunks to be alcoholic, nor do we have to be suffering signs of physical withdrawal from marijuana before we can be considered dependent. Even if neither tolerance nor withdrawal are present, by the time someone

- has lost control,
- tries, but can't stop,
- is preoccupied,
- neglects the rest of his or her life, and
- denies problems that are obviously being caused by the marijuana use,

he or she has become dependent on marijuana.

There is a reason that this section began with the question "What exactly is addiction?" and then proceeded to define "dependence" instead. Like many professionals in the chemical dependence field, I reserve the term *addiction* for others to apply to themselves when they are ready to acknowledge the truth about their relationship to alcohol or another drug. When people call themselves addicts, they are describing how their freedom has been lost and their lives have become committed to maintaining drug use. Addiction is the *experience* of being dependent.

Adolescents and Dependence

The DSM-IV criteria for chemical dependence provide a valuable framework for evaluating the relationship any individual has with alcohol or other drugs. There will be differences, of course, between adult and adolescent behaviors. Each age group has different responsibilities, different challenges, and different levels of maturity. Nevertheless, loss of control, preoccupation, inability to stop, neglect of responsibilities, and denial can occur at any age. Perhaps the biggest difference between adults and adolescents is the speed with which these criteria can appear and overtake a life.

Adolescents can progress from simple use of any psychoactive drug to full-blown dependence with frightening speed. What might take years in an adult can be collapsed into only a few months with teens. There are several reasons for this rapid development of dependence by adolescents: Their bodies, and thus their brains, are not yet fully developed. They have little backlog of experience to balance against intense drug-induced experiences. The pace of all psychological change is naturally fast during this important phase of development. And many adolescents still operate under an illusion of invulnerability, leaving them blind to any developing problems. Whatever combination of forces converge in adolescence, the appearance of enough behaviors to diagnose dependence often takes less than twelve months from the onset of use. Drug counselors commonly see thirteen- and fourteen-year-olds who were introduced to pot in the summer after eighth grade, sliding full speed down the academic tubes before Christmas in ninth grade. By then they may be buying a joint at school, intending to smoke it at night, but lighting up in the school bathroom before noon—loss of control.

Adolescents are likely to excuse out-of-control behavior as excitement at having scored or the natural response to being bored by a class or a teacher. They may swear off smoking during Thanksgiving vacation, when the family visits grandparents for a couple of days. But then they sulk the whole time about missing their friends (i.e., their smoking buddies), end up hiding between their earphones listening to music, thinking constantly about getting high again as soon as they get home, and smoking on the way to school the next Monday—inability to stop and preoccupation.

Homework becomes unimportant, as the student no longer cares about school—neglect of his or her life. And falling grades are seen as a rebellion against the system—a matter of maintaining integrity in the face of adult hypocrisy and efforts to control and stifle youth—denial.

Adolescents who are dependent on marijuana see pot as the only sensible response to the ridiculous pressures of the world. No arguments or facts to the contrary are considered. At this point, teens have developed sufficient dependence on marijuana that they may no longer be able to extricate themselves on their own. They need help if they are going to stop.

Marijuana Withdrawal

The DSM-IV criteria, it should be noted, do not require a person to have any symptoms of physical dependence (i.e., tolerance and withdrawal) to qualify for the diagnosis of chemical dependence. Three symptoms of psychological dependence are all that is necessary. Pot smokers generally reject the possibility of marijuana producing any physical dependence. And I must admit that I doubted the existence of any physical withdrawal symptoms for a couple of decades. During the nineties, my opinion changed when I began hearing long-term smokers describe a pattern of discomfort whenever they stopped smoking, especially if they had begun consuming better-grade pot with a higher concentration of THC. Disturbing evidence for physical dependence also began emerging from laboratories researching the brain's newly discovered endocannabinoid system.

The cannabinoid blocker SR141716A offers an excellent tool for demonstrating physical withdrawal from THC. Even though SR141716A blocks all cannabinoid activity, including the brain's own anandamide, animals tolerate the drug with little effect. However, when scientists administered THC to rats for several days at levels equivalent to what people ingest from smoking pot and then gave them SR141716A, the rats suddenly withdrew from the excess cannabinoid stimulation. A recognizable pattern of restlessness and irritability quickly followed. These are clearly symptoms of withdrawal, because rats that are given the blocker without having first been treated with THC show none of these reactions.

It is, of course, artificial to plunge an animal into sudden withdrawal from THC. Even heavy pot smokers withdraw slowly when they stop smoking, since considerable amounts of THC have been stored in their fat cells and leak out over a month or more. The practical significance of physical withdrawal from marijuana is certainly not dramatic, although it may have a subtle influence. Fully two-thirds of teenagers in treatment for marijuana dependence report experiencing some symptoms of withdrawal from pot. These symptoms, listed below, have a strong resemblance to the behaviors seen in rats that have been plunged into withdrawal in the laboratory. Many of the symptoms are also the opposite reaction to being high—similar to the way people feel in the aftermath of smoking. The most frequently reported symptoms of marijuana withdrawal include the following:

- restlessness
- irritability
- mild agitation
- sleep disturbances
- nausea or cramping or both
- fatigue

The question of whether marijuana can produce physical dependence is, therefore, not really a question anymore. Several lines of evidence all converge to prove that physical dependence does occur: (1) Animal models have demonstrated characteristic symptoms of abrupt withdrawal; (2) these symptoms correspond to clinical descriptions of withdrawal provided by teens in treatment; and (3) the brain's reward center reacts to marijuana in precisely the way it does to all other drugs of addiction. This third reason is important and fascinating enough to be explored in greater depth.

Dopamine and the Reward Center

The brain is affected in two ways by any psychoactive chemical upon which we become dependent. The first way, resulting from loss of receptor sites, has been described at some length. When marijuana, for example, causes enough of the brain's normal endocannabinoid receptors to be dismantled (in the brain's effort to reduce the effect of being flooded by THC), it leaves the brain less responsive to normal levels of anandamide. The relative inactivity of the endocannabinoid system following marijuana use leaves a person irritable, restless, and bored. The immediate antidote to these negative feelings is to smoke some pot and flood the remaining receptors with THC again.

An even more powerful change occurs in the brain's reward center, the *nucleus accumbens*. As described in the previous chapter, the reward center experiences an increase in the neurotransmitter dopamine in response to enjoyable activities such as dancing, eating a good meal, or having sexual experiences. This outflowing of dopamine is part of the physical mechanism of positive reinforcement to increase our interest in whatever activity stimulates the dopamine. We now understand the critical role the reward center also plays in addiction. Every drug that humans are known to abuse somehow causes a similar increase in dopamine, but often to higher levels than could ever be reached naturally. Nicotine, caffeine, alcohol, heroin, cocaine, amphetamine, Valium, and marijuana all stimulate from ten to a thousand times more dopamine in the reward center than any natural behavior observed in research animals. (There is no way yet to measure dopamine levels in humans during deep meditation or ecstatic states.) Penicillin, aspirin, and antidepressants such as Prozac do not cause an increase in dopamine. In essence, this rise in dopamine levels in the reward center has become one of the prime indicators for any drug's addictive potential.

Chronic exposure to THC in laboratory animals has been shown to change the actual structure of the reward center. On a cellular level, THC produces anatomic changes. It is likely that these brain changes produce the compulsive use of pot that underlies craving and loss of control. An interesting experiment was conducted on animals that had been given enough cocaine to become dependent. When the animals were put back in the test chamber where they had been given cocaine, the dopamine in their reward centers began rising spontaneously—before any drug had been given. Simply being exposed to the environment where cocaine had been experienced in the past caused the reward center to begin responding. Once the reward center has been modified by dependence on a drug, it seems to remember the cues associated with that drug and to reward even those cues. This probably underlies the tendency of recovering addicts to crave their drug of choice when exposed to the people, places, and things associated with their prior drug use.

I think of the changes THC and other drugs of abuse produce in the reward center as being similar to what happens to a balloon when it is first blown up. Before it has ever been expanded, the balloon is stiff and resistant. We have to puff our cheeks out and push with our lungs until the balloon finally begins to fill. After it has been expanded once, however, and the air let out, it is a lot easier to blow up again.

Something in the balloon has stretched, permanently. It will never go back to the *status quo ante*—the way it was before. This analogy helps one understand how changes produced in the reward center by dependence on any drug can leave a person primed to reactivate the addiction with even small amounts of drug use in the future.

The reward center also introduces us to intriguing interactions that exist between the endocannabinoid and endorphin systems. Although the full significance of the overlap between these two systems is still under investigation, anandamide and opiates have clearly been shown to have a unique relationship with each other. For example, both are involved in the control of pain (see chapter 12). Within the reward center, scientists can completely block the increase in dopamine caused by any opiate (e.g., morphine or heroin) by first giving the opiate blocker naloxone. Oddly, this opiate blocker also prevents the outflow of dopamine caused by marijuana, although it has no effect on any of the other drugs known to stimulate the reward center. We will have an opportunity to revisit this special relationship between endocannabinoids and endorphins in chapter 12 when we explore the current debate about medical marijuana.

A Commonsense Perspective

Because denial keeps adolescents from acknowledging that marijuana addiction is a possibility, let alone that it has happened to them, we often need to have a more palatable way of talking to them about their harmful involvement with pot. For pure simplicity and clarity, I like Andrew Weil's perspective on what constitutes an unhealthy relationship with a drug (*The Natural Mind* and *From Chocolate to Morphine*). No knee-jerk opponent of drug use, Dr. Weil has conceptualized four criteria that capture the essence of when a person is relating in an unhealthy manner to any drug, whether it be caffeine, Valium, marijuana, alcohol, heroin, tobacco, or any other chemical that affects the brain.[1] His criteria include the following:

- ignorance that the substance is a drug and of what it does to the body
- loss of the desired effect with increasing frequency of use
- difficulty separating from the drug
- impairment of health or social functioning

According to the first criterion, practically everyone in America using marijuana has an unhealthy relationship with it, since misinformation about how it affects the brain is so widespread. Because the information presented above is so new and has not generally been made available to the public yet, it is unfair to apply Weil's first criterion so broadly. More important is how many chronic marijuana users have their minds firmly made up about the value, and lack of harm, inherent in smoking pot. When people resist new information that challenges their perspective and when they rationalize their behavior on the basis that marijuana is natural, they probably meet Weil's first criterion for an unhealthy relationship to marijuana.

The "myth of natural" pervades our society in part because so many companies are making so much money from this myth. Commercials pitch products that are "all natural, so there are no side effects." Well, death cap mushrooms are all natural, too—even organic—but they will kill us nonetheless. Ephedra is sold as a natural herb, but most sports ban it as too dangerous. *Natural does not necessarily mean safe.*

The second criterion (loss of the desired effect with increasing frequency of use) is satisfied when smoking marijuana is frequent enough to become routine—part of getting ready for the day, preparing to have fun, or just dispelling boredom. At this point it is hard to argue that the drug is having the same effect as the first time it was used.

The smoker has grown used to its effects. Pot is no longer introducing the smoker to a new experience, but rather repeating a state of mind to which he or she is accustomed.

This same pattern may also represent increasing difficulty separating from pot, Weil's third criterion of an unhealthy relationship with the drug. Many people are not aware of crossing the line between having no interest in separating and having actual difficulty with stopping. For them, this third criterion is met more by the efforts they expend to assure that their supply of pot is not interrupted. Drug-seeking behavior is often an enjoyable activity in itself for adolescents who are excited by "the hunt" and feel a rush when they "score." But when excessive time and energy is put into maintaining their supply of weed, they have clearly fallen into an unhealthy relationship with pot.

Finally, impairment of function—socially, physically, financially, academically, professionally, legally, or spiritually—as a result of using any drug should be a clear sign of an unhealthy relationship. But this fourth criterion often looks quite different from the outside than it does from the inside. Many chronic pot users fail to see the impairments their use is causing. Often they blame the impairment on external factors, or they deny that the impairment is connected to the drug use. (*"You would use, too, if your parent treated you that way"* or *"School is so boring, you have to do something to put up with it."*) The most subtle impairments result from a slower than normal progression through school or career. Many smokers explain such impairments as the result of losing interest in meeting the standards society arbitrarily imposes on them, when in reality they usually result from not having learned the emotional coping skills necessary for adult life. Smoking is seen as a matter of maintaining self-esteem in the face of conformity.

From a parent's perspective, however, it can be painfully obvious when drugs have begun to derail a teen's life. "Loss of interest" in pursuing goals does not look like a change that truly emerged from the person's core because it actually grew in proportion to an increasing interest in smoking dope. Explanations for failures become lame, rationalizations that have little to do with the real reasons a teen's growth and maturation have been put on hold. Adolescents may protest more stridently than ever that they are capable of making their own decisions and taking care of themselves, if only they were given more freedom. The passion of their argument is powerful, but the logic seems woefully lacking. Any challenges to their point of view are seen as attacks. They talk defensively, and they continue to use in the face of impairments that are obvious to others. They have clearly entered into an unhealthy relationship with their drug, whether they can see this fact or not.

The Meaning of Addiction: Physical, Behavioral, Psychological

We are in a better position at this point to understand the meaning of addiction. On a physical level, addiction exists when the brain has laid down tracks that lead directly from a drug to large amounts of dopamine in the reward center. Once this has occurred, even thinking about pot is followed by an outflow of dopamine reward, and small amounts of smoking in the future lead to a quick reactivation of a full-blown dopamine response. On a behavioral level, addiction exists when an individual has lost control of use, is preoccupied with the drug even when not high, and does not see the problems created by using.

But it is on a psychological, more subjective level, that addiction has its most important meaning. Addiction is less about the reasons people begin using or why they become enthralled with a drug. It is more about the maintenance of drug use once it has become fully established in an individual's life. Addiction to marijuana exists when pot becomes a central organizing principle in one's life, the single most important thing to which an individual's life becomes committed. To be addicted means eventually to recognize one's enslavement. While grades and activities may be maintained for the time being, the individual stands ready to sacrifice other desires to maintain drug use. Addiction means subjugation, a profound loss of voluntary control. Once addiction exists, the individual has lost the capacity to control drug-using behavior by willpower alone. Surely willpower is still necessary to abstain, but it often becomes effective only when combined with outside support and help. Once addiction has been established, individuals lose any real sense of control over their lives (which has yet to fully form in adolescents to begin with). Their addiction has become more powerful than their better judgment.

Just how powerful is the addictive potential of marijuana? Best estimates are that approximately 10 percent of people who wait until they are at least eighteen years old before experiencing marijuana will become dependent at some time in their lives, roughly the same percentage as with alcohol. A much higher percentage of people who try nicotine, opiates, or stimulants such as cocaine and amphetamines eventually become dependent. A different picture emerges when adolescents under eighteen years old begin smoking marijuana. The younger teens are when they begin using marijuana, the greater their risk of developing abuse and dependence, the more quickly addiction will occur, and the more disruptive it will be to their lives.

The Risk of Addiction

The conclusion is simple, but scary. The risk of addiction to marijuana rises sharply with early onset of use. Any marijuana use by an adolescent entails risk, just as any automobile driving by teens necessarily entails risk. The younger one starts either, the greater the risk. This increased risk may be due as much to the inexperience and incomplete maturation of adolescence as it is to any pharmacological properties of pot. What does it matter? The fact is clear that risk increases with early marijuana use.

As I said at the beginning of this chapter, I have never seen a marijuana addict passed out in the gutter. On the other hand, I *have* seen fifteen-year-olds dissipating their lives in a haze of marijuana smoke. Despite losing long-term friends, failing in school, dropping out of sports, alienating their families, getting into legal difficulties, and falling into a morass of lethargic depression and hostility, they continue smoking. Despite failing to accomplish nearly all the developmental tasks of adolescence, including taking responsibility for their own health and future, they deny that marijuana is part of the problem. Instead, they blame every misery on outside factors and hold on tightly to their pot as their only succor, their only balm. They lie, cheat, steal, and manipulate to hide their use and do not see how this behavior destroys self-esteem. And very commonly, they eventually supplement, or supplant, their marijuana use with other drugs.

For these reasons, the 1.5 million teens between twelve and seventeen years old who began smoking marijuana in 1999 rises to the level of a true public health issue. We all have a stake in curtailing underage drinking, underage tobacco use, underage driving, and early adolescent marijuana use.

Chapter 4

Why Teens Begin Using Marijuana: The Seductive Power of Pot

Have you ever wanted to just get out from underneath all the pressures weighing on you, to stop the world for a few hours, to get away from the routine of who you have become, and to dream about what life could be? Have you ever wearied of having to take life's responsibilities so seriously, wanted to lighten up, take the afternoon off, laugh at your cares? Or are there times you wish you could be a little bad, let loose, and say the hell with trying to do what's right all the time, bend the rules, take some risks? Perhaps more important, have you longed for greater mystery in your life, a deeper curiosity about your connection to the infinite, even a spiritual transformation?

I certainly have felt all these things, and they help me relate to why many teens are attracted to experimenting with marijuana and drugs in general. As adults, we are under a constant barrage of "answers" to these longings: buy a lottery ticket, take a vacation, drive a sporty car, be sexy, order this brand of beer, catch the right mate, take yoga. The quick fixes are alluring, but superficial, and even adults are not always prepared to deal with all the marketing that touts easy answers. The longings are very real, and most of us are familiar with how much power they have. To understand why teens begin to play with pot, we need to understand that they have the same longings, without the experience to help them steer away from easy answers.

Underneath these longings are a host of motivations, most of which are completely natural.

Curiosity as a Fundamental Motivation

Adolescence is a time of tremendous change. Too often, adults and teens think the primary task of adolescence is separation. Many consider adolescent rebellion to be a necessary part of the separation process. Indeed, there is a need for teens to begin loosening the connections between themselves and their parents. But this separation is not the most important change required. Adolescence is also a time for forming *new* connections—to one's peers, to the world outside family, to one's sexuality, to the deeper experience of self coming into awareness, and to one's innate spiritual longings. Separation from family is necessary primarily to open up space for all the new connections teens must forge. Curiosity fuels the drive to find new relationships and to experience the world beyond the confines of home.

Adolescence is life's first really conscious voyage of discovery. Teens are aware that they are on a profoundly important voyage, and this conscious awareness helps in guiding the voyage. Some are terrified and try to remain moored to their home dock as long as possible. Others are cautious and take several short cruises first before striking out for more distant ports. Some respond to the challenge and sail out directly to find their fate, while others are so thrilled by the adventure lying just over the horizon that they charge out like dog soldiers high on adrenaline. Human temperament varies widely, making it nearly impossible to make any universal generalization about teenagers.

Still, we can be sure that the majority of teens who experiment with marijuana are motivated primarily by a desire to satisfy their innate curiosity about the world. Whether they first try pot with trepidation or rush headlong into the experience, they are intrigued by what lies ahead for them. It is one of a thousand ways they are trying on new parts of the world to see how each fits for them. While they may be ignoring or denying the risks, the motivation propelling them is essentially healthy.

Darker Motivations

In many cases, however, adolescents are motivated to try drugs more by a desire to get away from home than to reach any given destination. Poverty, whether emotional, spiritual, or financial, has parched their family and grown sharp thorns on what should be comforting relationships. Cruelty, whether emotional, spiritual, physical, or sexual, has scorched away any desire for family, leaving some kids to stow away on whatever ship they can find. Family problems often contribute tremendously to the urge to find solace in alcohol and other drugs.

Finally, some adolescents are so discomforted by their own sense of failure and internal distress that the distraction that drugs offer is too powerful to resist. Depression and anxiety can bedevil teenagers just as deeply as they torment adults. The stress that kids bear today is far beyond any that most of us experienced during our youth. Success in college seems to be predicated on getting into the correct kindergarten. No wonder that any hint of a learning disorder or attention deficit hyperactivity disorder (ADHD) plummets kids into feeling defective and doomed (see chapter 5). Whatever offers any hope of relief from these stressors is bound to be welcome.

All Dressed Up with No Place to Go

Adolescence, then, is a time of fundamental transformation in perspective, basic connections, and identity. Because this process of transformation takes place over several years, impatience and urgency are common, if not legendary, among teenagers. The experience of being "all dressed up with no place to go" pervades the adolescent's life, especially sexually. Having a driver's license but not owning a car symbolically defines the teen years. On a more abstract level, teens often have a fully formed concept of independence and freedom but still lack some of the basic tools to realize this goal. It is human nature for them to focus more on the barriers placed on their freedom than on the preparatory tasks that lie ahead of them.

It is within this maelstrom of powerful forces that drugs are first encountered, and their effects can be profoundly seductive. The French novelist Marcel Proust wrote, "The real voyage of discovery consists not in seeking new landscapes, but in having new eyes." I suspect that this advice applies more to wearied adults than to fresh teens, for whom seeking new landscapes is precisely their most important challenge. Their recently developed abstract thinking is all the new eyes they need. Now their job is to seek new landscapes that satisfy their own unique needs and desires and then to connect emotionally to these new vistas.

Marijuana provides much more of the "new eyes" that Proust describes than the "new landscapes" that teens need. Suddenly, with a minimum of effort, a little pot overlays the world with a superficial sense of novelty. Being high seems to transform everything and passively grants teens an experience of great connectedness. This new world is probably nothing like the one Mom and Dad live in, so an immediate sense of separation appears. Almost magically, marijuana seems to leapfrog an adolescent away from childhood. The chemically induced experience substitutes for actual, hard-won psychological development, and it can continue to substitute for emotional growth for years. While giving a teen an illusion of having jumped ahead in development, marijuana, like any drug, can actually delay and distort maturation. The chronic pot smoker may wake one day to find that peers have long ago embarked successfully into their adult lives, leaving him or her behind, without the skills required to move ahead.

Major Developmental Tasks

Let's look more closely at some of the developmental tasks facing adolescents and at how marijuana substitutes for successfully completing these tasks. Because individuals reach their teen years with different temperaments, inherent capabilities, and family experiences, they do not all face exactly the same challenges. Nevertheless, there are a set of developmental steps that nearly everyone has to take during the years between childhood and adulthood. The tasks teens have in common fall into the following areas.

Identity and Values

The question "Who am I?" is intensely, and often obsessively, important during the teen years. Centuries ago, this may not have been as difficult a question to answer. For most people, life was contained in a small geographic area, often one unchanging village, and survival demanded far more attention than did psychological development. Individuals generally absorbed their family's identity, largely because so few alternatives were available. Today, however, kids come into contact with influences from around the globe before they enter grade school. The choices are infinite, and there is plenty of time to try on multiple identities while preparing for adult life. The modern ethos emphasizes discovering the true self and not giving in to conformity. As a result, few teens are content simply to adopt their parents' identities.

Our sense of identity is largely determined by the values that guide our lives. We may value sports, the arts, or academics. We may value friends, achievement, or material wealth. We may value action or feeling, utility or beauty, victory or fair play, power or justice, dominance or honesty, toughness or gentleness. Adolescence is the time when teens emerge from being good primarily by minding the rules and begin developing more abstract and universal ideas to guide them. It is a time when adult hypocrisy is most disappointing and aggressively rejected. During adolescence, teens integrate a sense of identity by developing their own internal moral compass.

Peer Group

Family members are the most important people in a preadolescent's life. The very idea of being more tightly connected to someone outside the family than to blood relatives makes no sense to young kids. However, with puberty and the upwelling of sexual energies that are taboo to direct toward other family members, the importance of peers increases dramatically. Suddenly, allegiances and emotional attachments to others outside the home become intense and may seem to become primary. The influence of family fades and is resisted or suppressed. But this generates new problems for teens, who still need to be affiliated closely with someone. Which group of peers should they join? The "visible" group? The nerds? The jocks or the brains? The straights or the stoners? And will they be accepted by the group they desire? While family generally accepts the adolescent unconditionally, acceptance is not assured, nor is it constant and freely given, by peers, who are themselves groping for identity and connection. Unresolved adolescent issues are often intensified by the rapidly changing, still maturing social network being worked out by other adolescents. The question of choosing, and being chosen by, the "right" group of peers generates much of the stress found in today's teens.

The peer group an adolescent identifies with and the sense of identity he wants to try on are intimately related. As mutual attachments are forged and emotional commitments form between teens and their friends, their commonality reinforces how they view one another. A tendency to take studies seriously, for example, becomes a defining characteristic when shared with others. In the same way, disrespect for parents can be so strongly reinforced within a peer group that teens are embarrassed to feel any affection for us, much less display it publicly. Peer groups enhance aspects of teens' personalities, de-emphasize others, and lead children to try out behaviors that they would not otherwise try. These influences can be positive and negative. And none of us has much influence over which peers our children are attracted to.

Sexual Maturation

During adolescence sexual hormones begin rising up to take control of adolescents' bodies, as well as their emotions. No amount of practice prepares children for the reality of puberty. Dancing about like Britney Spears or the Spice Girls was just play, while new sensations and swelling in suddenly noticeable breast buds is real. Posturing like Arnold Schwarzenegger or some sports hero is just fantasy, while growing pubic hair and noticing the voice drop an octave is real. Looking at the other sex, really *looking*, and desiring something they can still only imagine makes it clear that they are not just kids anymore. They've got what every adult's got, and they understand that it feels good.

Puberty happens at its own pace for every adolescent. How much smoother it would all be if everyone experienced the same changes together, like when everyone moved at the same time from grade school to middle school. Instead, a few kids enter puberty first, and a few enter it last. As arbitrary as each individual's timing is, it nonetheless has a major impact on a teen's life and self-esteem to be either "too soon" or "too late." Being preyed upon, ridiculed, or admired on the basis of sexual development often greatly increases the need for acceptance.

Autonomy and Separation

For adolescents to make new connections with the world outside the family, they must complete two intertwined developmental tasks:

autonomy and separation. Each child emerges from the womb as more than a combination of qualities from Mom and Dad. We are each unique, with characteristics, drives, and urges that differ from those of our parents. Healthy families make room for, honor, and welcome the differences. But even in families that are not threatened by their children's own ways, each child has to discover and value all of who he or she is. Eventually, maturity demands that teens accept and take responsibility for their individual qualities, whether their parents do or not. This is autonomy.

Separation from family is eventually necessary for several reasons. Kids must leave home, emotionally and physically, to solidify their ability to take care of themselves. We must all prove our competence at navigating the world at large to know, really *know* deeply, that we have become adults. Only then can we return home and rework the relationship with our parents, adult to adult. No one else can make this transition for us. We have to do it ourselves, and we begin during our teen years.

Transcendence and Meaning

Finally, teens are often plagued by the need to begin making sense of the world and their lives. I say "plagued" because most of us eventually discover that our childhood understanding of life is no longer acceptable. As we become better able to think abstractly during adolescence, we begin to see more of the complexities of life. But, paradoxically, less and less of the world makes as much sense as it seemed to when we were younger and saw everything more simplistically. Many, if not most, teens feel betrayed by their confusion—betrayed because they had always thought parents knew what they were doing all the time and because they had always been assured that everything would be safe and okay. Now they discover that the world contains real injustice and evil, with no guarantees that good will triumph.

Adolescence is a time of immense spiritual challenge, for which a great many teens have had inadequate preparation. As a result, many teens feel adrift, without any clear sense of meaning in their lives.

Is there any significance to life beyond surviving, eating, sleeping, and reproducing? Does it add up to anything more than who gets the most toys before they die? As teens see more of the realities that they had been spared as youngsters, both by parents' desire to protect them and by their own inability to think abstractly, they react strongly. Some become cynical and bitter. Others wonder where justice can be found. And most still long for some of the certainty and clarity they had only a few short years ago. The desire to transcend the limitations and superficiality they see destroying life's meaning is strong during the teen years. Many hope that getting into adult life will bring some answers to the difficult questions that have stolen the last remnants of their childhood. Adolescents feel a strong drive to transcend their current life psychologically, physically, and spiritually. This drive strongly motivates their maturation.

Developmental Tasks for Parents

Before looking at how the experience of being high on marijuana can substitute for successfully completing developmental tasks, I want to take a moment to point out that as parents we face our own developmental challenges as our children pass through adolescence. After years of taking direct responsibility for managing the risks facing our children, we now need to begin stepping back. If teens are to begin taking greater responsibility for themselves, we have to make space for this to happen. Except in situations that threaten basic health and safety, we gradually have to move into the role of consultants to our kids' lives, where before we had been producer and director. The timing of this shift in roles is critical and difficult. While some of us turn too much freedom and responsibility over to our children too soon, others hold on too long. There is no perfection here, only trial and error.

Shifting into the role of consultant goes beyond a change in child-rearing techniques. It represents a developmental step for the parent as well. Impulses to overcontrol the world that went unchecked during our child's early life suddenly become the focus of intense power struggles with adolescents. To pick battles wisely, we parents need clarity about what lies under our control and what does not. We need to have enough self-worth to feel valuable to our children even when we've been relegated to the sidelines of their lives. It helps to be solid in our faith, whatever form that might take. Without faith that the universe provides the support teens need to mature into healthy adults, the next few years are going to be filled with anxiety. It is a rare parent who understands that anxiety about his or her teen is not the teen's fault. Anxiety about the normal process of separating from our partially-matured teenage child is our responsibility. It is not the child's job to soothe our fears or our dislike of "losing our babies."

Different Views on Why Teens Experiment with Drugs

The initial experimentation with smoking grass is often a watershed moment in a child's life. Despite all the antidrug messages received in school and at home, many teens and preteens decide to take the risk of getting high soon after the opportunity first presents itself. This single act is a clear step away from the path prescribed by most parents. In households where the importance of not using drugs has been emphasized, it is a direct act of disobedience. (We're ignoring for the moment kids who are introduced to smoking marijuana by their parents, either directly or by dipping into their parents' stash to get their first joint.) Trying marijuana for the first time is also an act of self-assertion. The child has weighed the issue, more or less carefully, and come to his or her own decision. At this point, teens do not doubt that they are charting their own course. They are claiming their freedom, and no one can control them. That's a fact.

An adolescent's decision to smoke marijuana is often seen very differently by the two sides—parents and kids. The disparity in how each perceives this moment is important, because it forms the framework for a lot of failed prevention programs and a lot of unsuccessful family discussions. Author David Wilmes asked each group why they believe kids use drugs and found some interesting differences (*Facts about Kids' Use of Alcohol and Other Drugs*). Adults gave the following reasons:

- School: "Can't those teachers see what's going on? Don't the kids get any supervision?"
- Other parents: "Well, what can you expect from a home like that?"
- Peer group: "My kids never had any problems till they got in with that bunch."
- Pushers or alcohol sales: "Put the pushers in jail and close up those sleazy places."
- Media: "What can you expect when the movies take it for granted that it's cool to use drugs?"
- Police: "If the cops were on the ball, they'd pick up those kids the first time they got out of line." Or "If the cops wouldn't hound the kids as if they were all criminals, they wouldn't even think of using drugs."
- Role models: "Those rock stars are all into drugs—just like professional athletes. And these are the people our kids want to imitate."

These reasons generally point to external factors. Perhaps parents are reluctant to believe that their children would willfully defy them unless they were being pressured by others. Parents tend to place great emphasis on peer pressure as the cause of adolescent drug use. As a result, programs designed to prevent drug use are heavily weighted toward helping kids resist peer pressure. This perspective is guided by the belief that drug pushers are lurking around every corner, waiting for our kids. Without these pushers, teens would follow their instincts and mind their parents.

But teens tell a different story. When asked why they think kids use drugs, teens gave the following reasons:

- "I wanted to see how I'd feel."
- "I wanted to be part of the group."
- "I didn't want to be a nerd."
- "I just wanted to have some fun."
- "I like to take risks."
- "I'm no baby. I can make up my own mind."
- "I like to experiment with new things."
- "I wanted to feel grown up."

Unlike adults' perspectives, these reasons are more internal. While teens may be underestimating the presence and power of peer pressure, they are also owning responsibility for their decisions to a degree greater than adults seem willing to give them credit for. This is completely consistent with the need teenagers have to take control of their lives. They are intrigued by the wide world, including sometimes by what the experience of being high would feel like, and they even enjoy the risk it might entail. No one thinks it odd when a teen courts the risk of rock climbing, sailboarding, or fast driving. These risky behaviors may make us nervous, but we see them as normal adolescent behavior, part of defining for themselves what their limits are. The impulse to experiment with marijuana has the same lure as other risky choices.

Understanding adolescents' perspectives is an important step to being able to communicate with teens. The temptations that attract them and the desires resident in their hearts form part of the cutting edge by which they learn their true identity. Adolescence is an important time for beginning to come to terms with adult desires. From this standpoint, teens are teaching us something important when they list the internal reasons for using drugs. As parents, however, we are often made nervous by the fact that this is occurring precisely when our kids are developing the capacity and freedom to satisfy these desires if they choose. And one simple, available, and relatively passive avenue for exploring their newfound desires is through experimenting with marijuana, alcohol, and other drugs.

Marijuana and Maturation

Marijuana confuses a teen's life by seeming to accelerate while actually delaying maturation. With one puff on a joint, the question "Who am I?" develops new answers, even before an adolescent gets high. "I am a risk taker. I am free from old constraints. I am not the child my parents still think I am." A line is crossed—a line between us and them. Now a teen is one of "them," fully distinguished from the person he or she was only a few moments ago. The excitement of the moment can be truly electrifying. A whole new peer group is joined. For many teens, the experience is like joining a secret society, complete with informal code words, insider expressions, and double meanings. Even straight experience seems altered as the new initiate walks through the next few days with an inner knowledge that no one else suspects. Parents, teachers, and other unsuspecting adults do not see the new truth. Maintaining an appearance of being unchanged can become a delicious deception. For once it is profoundly clear that the outside world does not know who they really are. For many teens, these feelings substitute for developing a more substantial sense of identity.

For most people, the first experiences with marijuana are pleasant (although a small percentage immediately dislike pot because they feel anxiety, loss of control, and even panic). What only a few minutes ago had been a source of fear, excitement, and anticipation (*"What will getting high really be like for me?"*) is quickly converted into a new playground, often filled with raucous laughter and silliness. The experience of getting high ends up being just plain fun for most, which suddenly throws all the dire warnings they had heard about marijuana into serious doubt. The smoking culture carries a set of values that are easily adopted by new smokers. Anyone seen as being antipot is now considered to be ignorant, oppressive, and hypocritical. Many teens feel adults have lied to them about drugs, and this feeling is inflamed by the new peer group they have entered. Stoners, as many teens committed to smoking pot call themselves, know the "truth" about marijuana; others are not to be trusted. The immediate acceptance into this new peer group brings a strong sense of belonging and at the same time drives a wedge between the teen and nonsmokers. The process of withdrawal from family, for the purpose of hiding and protecting marijuana use, has begun.

True autonomy requires developing the internal capacity to take responsibility for oneself. The pseudoautonomy of being high is less about being able to take care of oneself and more about being able to cast off parental control and identity. Few adolescent pot smokers see that parental controls remain central to their identity by virtue of defining themselves as rejecters of parental control. Getting high creates an impression for many teens that they are free, independent spirits, thinking and acting for themselves. No one can tell them what to do, and each joint they light up seems to reconfirm their freedom.

This illusion of independence gets played out in several different ways. Some kids overtly scoff at any attempts to corral them. They blatantly disobey parents, ignore school authorities, and come into conflict with police and the juvenile justice system. Throughout this process they seem to become progressively "radicalized." That is, as frustrated parents yell threats and attempt to clamp down with rigid controls, some teens feel increasingly justified in their alienation. As defeated school officials threaten expulsions, adolescents begin to feel increasingly cast aside by uncaring adults. As police bring the often clumsy, heavy hand of the law down upon them, pot smokers become more outraged at the hypocrisy and injustice of a system that wants to jail them while ignoring how often drunken parents get away with abusing their children. Those who most directly and overtly reject straight society are, in a sense, the most honest about their feelings, but they are also usually the least understood and most punished.

On the other end of the spectrum are those teens who quietly develop devotion to smoking pot without revealing a trace of their secret life. They maintain their grades. They maintain their behavior. But they have gone underground psychologically. They operate with an illusion of independence as they live progressively more in their fantasies than in reality. These kids are the hardest to really know. Naturally tending more toward introspection than toward action, they are often attracted by the sense of transcendence offered by the "magical" powers of cannabis.

Michael Pollan, in his enjoyable book *The Botany of Desire*, points out that transcendence "depends for its effect on losing oneself in the moment." Marijuana's tendency to disrupt memory and slow the perception of time mimics transcendence. To some people, this can be disturbing. They become uncomfortable with the mild disorientation created by the mental discontinuities that occur. Others find the experience hilarious. They enjoy being bumped "outside the box" of their normal patterns of thinking and believe that the experience enhances creativity. While most of the "amazing" ideas that appear while high are neither practical nor well remembered in the cold light of the next morning, the astronomer Carl Sagan, in his article "Mr. X," believed that he benefited from occasional visits to the altered consciousness created by smoking marijuana.[1]

In addition, marijuana has been used in spiritual pursuits by a wide range of cultures over many millennia. When the transcendent-seeming experience of marijuana's high combines with the intensification of sensory experiences, virtual novelty, and sense of awe produced by stimulating the amygdala with THC, a powerful chemical cocktail results, one that takes people out of their day-to-day experience and gives them a taste of the transcendent.

Many adolescents quickly become enthralled by the experience of being high. Away from their humdrum lives, away from the challenges and responsibilities of school, family, and preparing to meet an uncertain future, they can be entranced by the strange world of high possibilities. This is not true spirituality, but it does kick people out of their normal ways of relating to the world. It does say there is a universe of other possibilities, although it does not help to *realize* any of them. To adolescents, who lack the experience useful for resisting such temptations, marijuana may seem to be the key that unlocks their way into a different world. They make the common error that Alan Watts, in *The Wisdom of Insecurity*, described as looking at the finger pointing the way and then sucking it for comfort rather than following it. There is a universe of possibilities open to teens, and this is a good thing to know and believe. But the task is to *enter* that world in reality, not merely to look at it in fantasy.

The effect of marijuana use during the adolescent years is all too often to delay and distort psychological, emotional, social, and spiritual development. The younger an adolescent is when beginning to smoke pot, the more the resulting developmental delays and distortions cascade through his or her personality, building a momentum that extends the negative consequences far into the future. When adulthood is built on a poor foundation, the effects can reverberate for a lifetime.

In addition, the earlier an adolescent begins smoking marijuana, the higher the risk he or she runs of becoming enthralled and seduced by the experience. For many, seduction soon gives way to devotion, and addiction is not far away. To be addicted (from Latin *ad dictare*) means to address one's entire life to that substance. Everything else in one's world, and in one's psychology, is subordinated to obtaining, using, or recovering from using the drug. Not all kids are equally susceptible to being seduced or developing addiction to marijuana. Some run a much higher risk for reasons that have nothing directly to do with pot. The next chapter looks at the risk factors that place some teens in greater danger than their peers.

Chapter 5

High-Risk Teens:
The Unequal Distribution of Risk

Life is not fair, and the inequality of life as it relates to addiction is significant and multilayered. There are genetic differences at the core of every cell. There are neurological differences peppered throughout our brains. And there are profound environmental differences, including the families we are born to, the neighborhoods surrounding our families, and the culture surrounding those neighborhoods. All these influences powerfully affect our overall life experience financially, socially, educationally, spiritually, and physically. And they also powerfully affect any individual's risk of developing chemical dependence.

While each decision to use marijuana is an individual choice, with the individual (and his or her family) mainly bearing the consequences of that choice, society as a whole is, in part, responsible. What hurts any individual hurts us all eventually. We all feel the impact when individuals at high risk for addiction experiment with marijuana and end up paying a high price. For example, adolescent marijuana use has been shown to increase the risk of not graduating from high school; delinquency; having multiple sexual partners, with a consequent higher rate of contracting HIV; and suicidal behavior—all of which tax community resources.

The Chicken-and-Egg Conundrum

Researchers encounter an interesting conundrum when they try to understand the relationship between kids, marijuana, and problems typical of adolescence. Troubled teens (e.g., school dropouts, delinquents, runaways, attempted suicides) have a much higher than average rate of marijuana use than other teenagers. On the other hand, youth who smoke marijuana experience a higher rate of problems (e.g., increased risk of later substance use behaviors, conduct/oppositional disorders, juvenile offending, severe truancy, dropping out of school, anxiety, depression, and suicidal ideation). The rates of these various problems range between three and thirty times greater for teens who begin smoking pot before age fifteen. In other words, kids with problems are more likely to use marijuana, and kids who use marijuana are more likely to have problems. It is not always clear which is the chicken, which is the egg, or which came first. The only general conclusion that can be drawn is that abusing marijuana and a wide range of adolescent problems frequently go hand in hand. That much is certain.

The Risk Factors

Adolescents who have been harmfully involved with marijuana often say that they began smoking at the same time as several of their friends. But even though everyone made the same initial choices, their friends didn't smoke as much or didn't continue smoking as frequently. The following sections explore the factors that are responsible for the different consequences individuals experience from the same choices.

Genetics

The most fundamental risk factor for marijuana addiction (and addiction in general) is genetics. Genetic susceptibility to addiction forms a firm cornerstone of our current understanding of addiction as a disease. The single most powerful predictor of any individual's risk for developing addiction is a positive family history—a parent, grandparent, uncle, or aunt who is chemically dependent.

The evidence establishing genetics as an important risk factor comes from several different directions. Genetic influence was first established for alcoholism and is now being extended to marijuana addiction. Studies of genealogies have shown that alcoholism clusters in families, even when family members live far apart from each other. Studies of identical and fraternal twins, who share 100 percent and 50 percent of the same DNA, respectively, have shown that the more DNA shared with a family member who is alcoholic, the greater the likelihood that a person will also develop alcoholism. Studies of children of alcoholics who are adopted at birth into nonalcoholic families have shown that they run the same high risk of becoming alcoholic. Conversely, if a child whose natural parents are not alcoholic is adopted by an alcoholic parent, his or her risk of developing alcoholism is no higher than if he or she had been raised by a nonalcoholic. So we know that increased risk is transferred largely through the genes we inherit, not through childhood experience alone. And finally, strains of mice have been found that voluntarily drink alcohol to excess, while other strains avoid alcohol. In a similar vein, we now have strains of mice that self-administer THC and others that do not. We also have found strains of mice that do not show the typical dopamine increase in the reward center when they are administered THC. Clearly, there are genetically determined differences in our susceptibility to marijuana addiction, just as there are genetically determined differences in how people's brains respond to alcohol.

As a result of genetic influences, some kids take to marijuana like a duck to water, or like an alcoholic to beer. The same amount of smoking has a more immediate and profound impact on them than on their peers. In the words of Bill W., a cofounder of Alcoholics Anonymous (AA), when referring to the first time he tried alcohol, "Lo, the miracle! That strange barrier that had existed between me and all men and women seemed to instantly go down."[1] These words could apply as well to the welcome reception some people give to their first marijuana high. The reward they experience from flooding the endocannabinoid system in the brain with THC seems to be far greater than average. A sense of calm and belonging descends upon them. If, for any reason, their lives are in greater turmoil than those of their peers, the sense of calm and belonging is even more welcome. On the basis of their genetically-programmed brain chemistry, they run a higher risk of eventually becoming harmfully involved with pot. Their risk of addiction is greater, through no fault of their personality.

Parental addiction is not a sure predictor of who will become harmfully involved with pot. Not all children, not even the majority, with addicted parents become addicted. And teens with no known family history of addiction certainly can become addicted. But if we had only one question to ask to find the group of adolescents who run the highest risk of problems with marijuana, it would be to ask who has a parent who is abusing, or dependent on, any chemicals.

Living with an Abusing or Addicted Parent

Not only are teens with an abusing or addicted parent at greater risk for inheriting a genetic predisposition to addiction, but living with a parent who is harmfully involved with alcohol or other drugs also teaches a host of lessons. It teaches that adults normally respond to emotional distress by resorting to chemicals. It recruits kids into the same denial that already shrouds the parent from the truth about his or her illness. It teaches kids to hide the truth from the world outside the family, to lie, to cover their family shame, and to remain "loyal" to a parent by acting as though nothing is wrong.

Living with an addicted parent can also teach kids that nothing in the world is really predictable. It teaches children that they are ultimately on their own. No one can ever be counted on to protect them. Chaos and despair simply need to be lived with. Emotional needs come second. It teaches many kids to harden their hearts and not let anyone in, to avoid being hurt even further. It teaches children not to trust.

Some kids living with an addicted parent learn to become caregivers. One survey of social workers found that nearly half had an alcoholic parent. While learning to be a caregiver is a valuable skill, being recruited into this role too early in life can also create problems. Alcoholic or other drug-addicted parents can lead their children to feel responsible for their care—responsible even for their illness. A deep sense of shame and inadequacy is often the legacy of trying to accomplish the impossible task of controlling, or curing, a parent's addiction.

Too often, addicted parents also fail to demonstrate that there is a way out of addiction. Children coming from addicted families may not understand that recovery is possible. If they should ever begin to slide toward addiction themselves, they can quickly succumb to a sense of the inevitable. For them, addiction is a black hole from which nothing emerges. It is a one-way path. And if an addicted teenager's parents have not found recovery, it dims the possibility that such a path would be available for the child.

Finally, a number of parents who are addicted actually introduce their children to using alcohol and other drugs. Sometimes the introduction is inadvertent, merely by passing out or carelessly leaving some marijuana unattended on the coffee table. Other times the joint is passed directly from father or mother to child. Addicted parents see their children through a lens that is deeply distorted by their drug use.

Through this lens, the boundaries between adult and child are blurred, or obscured. By smoking together, the addict sees the family as being closer. Being a friend is confused with being a parent. What teen in this situation could sort through all the lessons being taught and accurately reject those that are dangerous to his or her future?

Presence of a Psychiatric Problem

A third important risk factor for adolescent problems with marijuana is the presence of a separate psychiatric problem, such as attention deficit hyperactivity disorder, clinical depression, conduct disorder, social anxiety, post-traumatic stress disorder, or specific learning disorders. A psychiatric problem, very often preceding any drug use, can be found in 83 percent of teens who satisfy the criteria for marijuana dependence, in 46 percent of those with marijuana abuse, and in only 29 percent of occasional users.[2] In some cases, teens may use marijuana in an effort to cope with underlying problems; in other cases, smoking can trigger the onset of psychiatric difficulties. In either case, being high usually intensifies psychiatric problems. In general, more severe psychiatric problems and more severe marijuana addiction are associated with one another.

Attention Deficit Disorder

Attention deficit disorder (ADD) is one of the most common problems I see in teens with marijuana dependence. They generally come into my office convinced that pot is the perfect medicine for their disordered attention span. The two effects of marijuana that they cite as benefits are that it calms them down (physically and emotionally) and it focuses their attention. Then they usually throw in, "It's all natural and God's gift to humans. Besides, the drugs doctors use are unnatural and have more harmful side effects." From their defense of marijuana, I can tell that they have gone beyond being seduced by its effects and have become devoted to its use. For teenage boys, especially, with hyperactive forms of ADD, marijuana is most often the drug of choice because their physical hyperactivity is often the primary cause of classroom problems.

The reality is that these kids with ADD are often half right. Pot does tend to calm their hyperactivity. Remember that our endocannabinoid system helps regulate our baseline level of spontaneous motor activity. Flooding this system with THC makes animals physically quieter, even nearly catatonic. I believe many of my ADD patients who say that they can relax better when they are stoned. They probably also feel emotionally less anxious. The terrible underlying sense of urgency that bedevils so many people with ADD is also considerably relieved by marijuana.

The reality is also that pot does nothing to improve the ADD sufferer's fundamental problem with concentration. I use a standardized computer test called the *Connors CPT* to help diagnose ADD. This fifteen-minute test measures several variables of attention, including reaction speed, impulsivity, distractibility, consistency, and the ability to sustain effort and performance. On several occasions I have had patients with ADD, documented by the *Connors CPT*, retake the test after getting high. They all report feeling they have performed far better. None of them, however, shows the slightest objective improvement. While marijuana *does* appear to decrease hyperactivity, it does *not* treat attention deficit disorder. In addition, its side effects are far more complex and potentially more far-reaching than those of the pharmaceutical drugs used to treat ADD.

With ADD, the basic problem appears to be the sudden collapse of activity in the brain's frontal lobe precisely when it normally should become more active during a concentration task. This area, called the prefrontal cortex, does not have a particularly dense concentration of anandamide or the cannabinoid receptor. Therefore, we would not expect THC to have a major impact on the cause of ADD, and it doesn't. Teens with ADD probably experience the same virtual novelty that all people do when their amygdala is overstimulated by THC. It is entirely possible that this experience is even more dramatic and fascinating for those who suffer from ADD, since they have been struggling for much of their lives to alter their ability to focus attention. The thrill of smoking pot may lie in the experience of being able to modify their poorly controlled attention.

Research has confirmed that adolescents with ADD (approximately 5 percent of the population) experience a higher rate of substance abuse, earlier substance abuse, and longer substance abuse than adolescents without ADD. Very important, however, is the discovery that proper medical treatment of ADD reduces the risk of drug abuse by a remarkable 85 percent. ADD is one risk factor for marijuana abuse and dependence that we can influence by early detection and treatment.

Depression

Depression is now recognized as common among adolescents. The National Institute of Mental Health (NIMH) estimates that 8 percent of teens suffer from depression. Fully three million teens meet the criteria for a diagnosis of clinical depression. The darkness, irritability, and despair they experience grinds no less deeply than in adults suffering from depression. Unfortunately, teen depression is less often recognized, because sufferers are usually not in a position to seek medical/psychological help on their own and adults have difficulty distinguishing their symptoms from the emotional volatility normally seen in adolescents. Those whose depression stems from childhood trauma —physical, emotional, and/or sexual—may even avoid seeking the professional help they need in order to protect family members who perpetrated the abuse. For these kids, the feelings of isolation and alienation that are an inherent part of depression are intensified by their family's denial.

A host of other factors leads to the overwhelming level of stress experienced by teens and their families today. Parents who work long hours or who are unable to find enough work to provide a secure home can stress teens as well. Divorce, single parenting, and remarriages can all create tension in kids. Competition for good colleges, good high schools, and even for the "best" kindergartens has robbed childhood of much of the down time that it used to have. Stranger abductions, the latest missing children on the nightly news, and terrorism on our own shores surround teens with an atmosphere of fear. Washboard abs, thin runway models, and perfect skin all seem necessary for acceptance. If teens *aren't* stressed out, some of us may wonder what's wrong with them. The demands put on hurried teens today and the unrealistic expectations they hold for themselves have produced levels of stress, and therefore levels of depression, unseen in past generations.

When depression is not recognized or treatment is not available, marijuana often is. The temporary mood elevation that comes with getting high is a relief to some adolescent sufferers of depression. But the elevated mood soon becomes more a memory than a reality. After the high wears off, the emotional slump that follows adds its weight to the underlying depression. They continue to smoke pot in hopes of recapturing the initial euphoria they experienced. As with all drugs, however, the first experience is never quite recaptured. Even when this search is in vain, depressed adolescents continue to see benefits in smoking. The buffer of sensations that results from a period of virtual novelty can be a welcome distraction. Combine this with marijuana's disruption of memory, especially negative memories, and isolated teens have a powerful balm for the arid inner feelings of depression. If they are lucky, sharing the high with friends may even dispel their sense of isolation for a few moments of artificially stretched-out time. Teens suffering depression are at increased risk of becoming harmfully involved with marijuana.

As with so many other drugs that temporarily seem to dissolve depression, or at least to draw a curtain over it, marijuana's high is usually followed by the opposite reaction. Just as alcohol, cocaine, heroin, speed, and a host of other drugs ultimately deepen and prolong the very depression that they temporarily lift, marijuana contributes more to maintaining depression in the long run. I have often found that the SSRI (selective serotonin reuptake inhibitor) antidepressants (e.g., Prozac, Paxil, Zoloft, Celexa), which are usually so helpful, fail to make a significant dent in the depression of a person who is also exposing his or her brain to THC. Remember that the endocannabinoids work largely by modifying the brain's sensitivity to other neurotransmitters. Unbalancing the natural brain chemistry at the cannabinoid level makes other pharmacological interventions less effective. In many, if not most, cases, only after people stop their marijuana use does the antidepressant they are taking begin to work fully—if it is even still needed.

Temperament

It is not only an inherited genetic susceptibility for addiction, parental substance abuse, and underlying psychiatric difficulties that increase an adolescent's risk of marijuana abuse. Temperament can play a role as well, especially the degree of risk aversion (i.e., caution) or risk taking that each child is born with. Just as genes heavily influence height and skin tone, they also influence several behaviors. Some children are born with a great ability to regulate themselves. They quickly fall into routine patterns of sleep, wakefulness, and eating. Other children have difficulty from the very beginning achieving such regularity. Some are easily aroused and easily soothed, while others require lots of stimulation to become disturbed and do not settle down easily. All of these behaviors seem to result from a combination of psychology and physiology. Somehow this combination also leads to some children tensing up and being scared easily, while others delight in excitement. The first may cry in distress when tossed into the air. The second giggles loudly and can't be thrown high enough to be satisfied; more is always better.

Human beings owe a great deal to individuals who are risk takers. Without them, we might still be waiting for someone to climb the highest mountain, to try riding in a powered glider, or to begin experimenting with electricity. Risk takers have led us in countless ways into important discoveries. Undoubtedly, many have also crashed and burned in the process. The child who climbs to the highest branch of a tree before looking to see if he or she can get down is probably no different in temperament from the explorer who sets off on skis to cross the South Pole. Sometimes the branch breaks, and sometimes the explorers never return.

High risk takers are more likely to experiment with marijuana and to experiment at earlier ages than others. With early onset of marijuana use comes a higher rate of eventually developing dependence. Therefore, the temperamental quality of caution is a protective factor vis-à-vis drug abuse, while high risk takers are, well, at high risk. Delaying use decreases risk.

An interesting relationship exists between first marijuana use and first alcohol or tobacco use for adolescents. Researchers have found that whichever of the alcohol-tobacco-marijuana triad is first encountered, the other two are highly likely to follow within the next year. This triad is therefore of particular danger to high risk takers. Once they have been intrigued enough to try a cigarette, or perhaps a beer, they are automatically at much higher risk of soon experimenting with marijuana as well. Whenever we see an adolescent walking down the street, cigarette in hand, we can assume he or she is at increased risk of trying a joint. Early alcohol and tobacco use greatly increase the risk of marijuana use as well.

Environment
Certain aspects of an adolescent's family environment have been identified as increasing the risk for early and heavy marijuana use.

Family Values
Families with moralistic, rigid, and extreme views about alcohol and other drugs breed more drug use by their children than do families with moderate views. This is true whether the extreme views favor or oppose drug use. In either case, the family has invested chemicals with a lot of emotional charge, and this charge gets passed on to their children. Moderation breeds moderation. Extremes increase risk.

Families that maintain their rituals and celebrations experience less drug abuse among their children. Routines such as family meals, vacations, and even shared regular chores create cohesion and provide ballast for youngsters. Families that maintain connections to their spiritual heritage and provide their children with some spiritual training decrease the risk of drug abuse. Celebrations of birthdays, anniversaries, and national holidays increase a sense of being important and honored in one's family. And cultural rituals such as those surrounding Christmas, Hanukkah, Kwanza, reunions, weddings, and funerals all help children feel connected to a broader world.

Supply versus Demand
Oddly enough, the ready availability of marijuana does not necessarily increase an adolescent's risk of marijuana abuse. To illustrate the lack of direct relationship between marijuana availability and use we need only look at two trends. In 1978, approximately 50 percent of

high school seniors had smoked pot during the previous twelve months. This fell to less than 25 percent by 1991 and has since risen to just shy of 40 percent. Throughout this entire time, however, the number of seniors who reported that it was easy to obtain pot held steadily between roughly 82 to 86 percent as shown in figure 6.

Figure 6: Trends in Perception of Availability

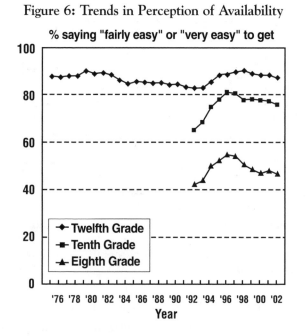

This figure illustrates the percentage of high school seniors from 1976 to 2002 who reported that it was either "fairly easy" or "very easy" to obtain marijuana. Eighth and tenth graders were surveyed beginning in 1991. (Courtesy of Monitoring the Future, Institute for Social Research, University of Michigan)

What *has* varied with increases and decreases of marijuana use is people's perceptions of its harmfulness. See figure 7 on page 90.

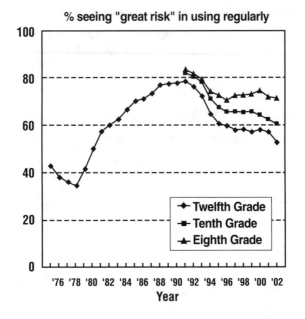

Figure 7: Trends in Perception of Risk

% seeing "great risk" in using regularly

This figure illustrates the percentage of high school seniors from 1976 to 2002 who saw regular use of marijuana as involving "great risk." Eighth and tenth graders were surveyed beginning in 1991. (Courtesy of Monitoring the Future, Institute for Social Research, University of Michigan)

The more harmful people see marijuana to be, the fewer people smoke, despite its unchanged availability. In other words, demand reduction appears to be more effective than supply reduction.

Community Norms

The community norms surrounding adolescents can have a profound impact on whether they try marijuana. While many communities want drug prevention to be taken care of at the schools, the problem is not isolated to school-age children. When communities wink at the adults' use of marijuana or tolerate other drug usage, the children absorb this message. Kids really do what their parents do, not what they say. Kids only pretend to do what parents say so they can do what parents do behind their backs. Nearly every community across America contains an adult drug-friendly subculture. Near my hometown, out on the Pacific Coast, lies an isolated community of old hippies. I have heard kids from that community complain when they were arrested for marijuana possession that they did not know it was illegal. Few, if any, in their home community ever object to its use or treat it as illegal.

While this is an extreme example, it illustrates a reality that exists in lesser forms in every community. I know too many lawyers, doctors, police officers, teachers, and school board members who still occasionally smoke marijuana not to understand that its use pervades every community. Trying to delay or prevent marijuana use among teenagers cannot be divorced from the community's norms as a whole. Without involvement of the whole community, school-based drug prevention programs are both hypocritical and doomed to be ineffective. The entire community has a stake in delaying and preventing teen use of marijuana. And the community's norms are a prime component of what must be openly discussed if this goal is ever to be reached.

The power of norms, and of kids' perceptions of the norms, was illustrated when I participated in surveying sixth, seventh, and eighth graders in a local middle school. (More than 65 percent of students voluntarily took the anonymous survey, which researchers had proven to be sufficient participation to provide valid results.) The percentage in each class who had ever smoked marijuana was reported at 0 percent for the sixth grade, 3 percent for the seventh grade, and 9 percent for the eighth grade (all below the state average in California). However, when asked how many of their peers they believed have ever smoked marijuana, a tremendous discrepancy became apparent.

Sixth graders believed that 40 percent of their peers had tried marijuana; seventh graders believed 51 percent had tried it; and eighth graders believed 75 percent of their peers had used marijuana! The norm was clearly to be a nonsmoker. But students *believed* the norm was to have experienced pot. The kids were flabbergasted when they learned these results. But without having their misperceptions corrected, it is easy to understand how their beliefs could become self-fulfilling prophecies. Environmental factors have a profound influence on risk.

When the same survey conducted at the high school found an increase in marijuana and other drug use, the school board was concerned, but voices were raised arguing that the results would alarm parents if made public. Clearly, not everyone was ready for an honest and frank discussion of the community's norms. When communities shy away from asking basic questions about what standards they want to promote to protect the health and safety of adolescents, they increase the risk that drug and alcohol use will be perceived as the norm.

The Media

A level of apathy has overtaken many communities as a result of the tremendous power of advertising and the media to permeate children's lives. This topic has already filled whole books. To provide one concrete example of the influence of marketing that is tolerated in nearly every community, I have a routine before addressing the school parent group each year. On the way to the talk, I stop at the supermarket that is within easy walking distance of both the middle and high schools. I go to the cold drink section, and every year I find bright, shiny alcohol-containing wine coolers on display, *touching* cans of name-brand soft drinks. "Training drinks" is what experts in environmental prevention call these wine coolers, 35 percent of which are consumed by underage drinkers. And we simply tolerate this seduction of youngsters. We tolerate it by not even noticing that it is occurring (because it is so pervasive we become inured to it). And we tolerate it because we either believe there is nothing we can do to change corporate behavior or because we fear the reaction of others if we object to having our children so blatantly targeted. Community norms create or diminish risk. In most communities, we are passively permitting marketers and the media to set the norms.

In conclusion, we need to recognize that not all kids are at equal risk. Even though the average risk for problems with marijuana is 10 percent for those who wait until they are eighteen or older before any experimentation (and progressively higher for every year under eighteen), some individuals are at much greater than average risk. The next step is to know how to recognize the signs of a teen who is truly getting into trouble with marijuana.

Chapter 6

Teens in Trouble with Marijuana: When Health and Safety Become Issues

Now things become really personal. Now it's no longer about abstract ideas of addiction or statistics about adolescents in general. Now it's about our own flesh and blood, our own teenager, or possibly one of our brother's or sister's children, or maybe one of our child's good friends. Most parents, somewhere within a circle that goes no farther than family and close friends, will know someone who gets into trouble with marijuana, alcohol, or other drugs. Every community contains teens who have slipped over the invisible line between using pot and becoming addicted to the point of having overwhelming legal, scholastic, family, and health problems.

As with all problems, early detection and intervention are preferable. But how can we know if we are only overreacting out of our own parental fears? How do we know that using pot is really causing any problems? And even when our fears are justified, how do we know the best time to act? This chapter provides useful guidelines for recognizing when a teen, unlike the majority of teens who experiment, is developing serious problems with marijuana. Later chapters address how to respond once we do become convinced our help is needed.

Barriers to Recognizing Trouble

A major barrier to recognizing when teens get into trouble with marijuana is the difficulty adults have distinguishing mood and behavior changes that are the result of drug use from the mood and behavior changes that naturally characterize this age period. The pace of normal change is rapid, and most kids become more volatile emotionally as they become teenagers. Their moods, and their personality as a whole, usually become more labile. What we see one day, or one minute, is often not what we see the next day or the next minute. Sometimes we can see the reasons for these sudden changes, but often we cannot. It is as though something has come unhinged within and swings about wildly with the slightest provocation. Periods of sullenness may descend without warning. Some teens withdraw into nonverbal grunts. Others ignite in explosive emotions and hostility that seem wholly uncharacteristic of who they have been for the previous decade. If we as parents are so easily baffled by all these changes, imagine how confusing it must be for the adolescent. We need to remember, if we can, our own adolescence.

Something *has* come unhinged within. Childhood no longer has them entirely in its grasp. Adulthood still only beckons them. Hormonal swells and sudden torrents are remolding their bodies. Why should their emotions be immune to such powerful influences? Change is the only constant in a teenager's life.

But adolescent development does have a trajectory. Like the Dow Jones average in a rising market, the trend is in a definite direction, even though the moment-by-moment, day-by-day fluctuations obscure the fundamental trend. Adolescent development is in the general direction of establishing an independent identity, more mature values that are reflective and supportive of that identity, mutual relationships with a group of peers, sexual maturity, sufficient responsibility to separate from family, a sense of meaning, and a more spiritual connection to the surrounding world. If a teen is not headed in this direction, something is interfering with the trajectory.

Understanding the Progression toward Dependence

As teens gradually get into trouble with marijuana, the trajectory of adolescent development changes. Marijuana use may delay, distort, fragment, or abort psychological development. It can lead a child to prematurely leap over necessary developmental steps, weakening the foundation needed to meet the later challenges of adulthood success-fully. During a period when change is the norm, disruptions in the trajectory of normal development are the major signs that a teen is getting into trouble with marijuana. The advent of addiction interferes enough with the normal trajectory of adolescent development to produce a pattern of behavior that can be recognized if parents are alert, willing to see the whole pattern, and clear about their role as parents.

The following framework will help parents recognize and understand signs that a child is getting into trouble with marijuana. Full-blown addiction does not appear on the scene all at once. People pass through a predictable progression as they become dependent on any drug. Although we can divide this progression into recognizable stages, there is not a sharp demarcation at the end of one stage and at the beginning of the next. The slide into addiction is seamless from stage to stage. Further confusing parents is the intermingling of this progression with other, normal adolescent behaviors. It helps to look first at what a teen experiences when becoming dependent on marijuana.

Learning the Mood Swing

The first step toward becoming harmfully dependent on marijuana almost always involves *curiosity*. Before they tried marijuana, users did not know what smoking pot would feel like. They were naive. They saw depictions of people getting high on television and in the movies. They heard thousands of references to getting high on the radio, by DJs and artists. Their friends joked about it. And possibly either they, or one of their peers, had an older neighbor or sibling or other relative who used pot and talked about it. They have probably even had access to pot. Opportunity and curiosity have a way of finding each other.

A willingness to take a *risk* has to be present along with curiosity. As much as young people minimize and deny any risk from pot smoking, nearly every new initiate feels anxious as the moment nears. *"How will I respond? Will I freak out? What will it be like?"*

Ultimately, we have to realize that most of us want our children to be curious and to have some willingness to take risks. We may have even encouraged these traits when we could. It is important not to demonize the normal impulse kids feel to push the envelope and try out new and interesting experiences. I can easily remember my own curiosity as a young adult when marijuana first became available to me through an old and trusted friend. The courting of risk was more exciting than scary, like facing a rock wall I was about to challenge. These are all normal feelings that in many situations are tempered by enough caution so that risks are properly managed.

In the great majority of cases, the effects of marijuana are quickly enjoyed. A striking alteration in consciousness follows the first awkward inhalations, often accompanied by whole body sensations, a shiver maybe. The seeming "harmlessness" of being high soon becomes apparent, and the experience becomes pleasant and playful, often hysterical. It may feel like recess in grade school—just plain fun. The adolescent has learned the mood swing produced by marijuana and, like most people, enjoys it.

The actual experience people have when first smoking marijuana stems not only from the effects of the drug but also very much from a combination of their expectations and the environment (called *set* and *setting*). When people expect to enjoy pot, they are more likely to have a pleasant experience. The more relaxed the setting, the better the experience. When a young person is talked into trying pot against his or her better judgment and when the atmosphere is tense because of a risk of getting caught (e.g., smoking in a friend's bedroom when his or her parents are in the house), the experience is likely to be colored by anxiety. On the whole, however, most kids remember their first experiences with marijuana fondly.

Seeking the Mood Swing

Adolescents who are simply experimenting with marijuana quickly find its intrigue fading. It either falls away from their lives after a few experiences or else drops into place as occasional, truly recreational, use. Their curiosity has been satisfied. There is no great attraction to repeating the risk.

But others find that they are more attracted to smoking marijuana than ever before. Marijuana is no longer a matter of curiosity. They are now actively seeking the mood swing. This attraction is often propelled by a *lack of emotional safety* somewhere in their lives. Sometimes the source of their lack of safety is obvious—arguing or divorcing parents, delayed or premature puberty, academic difficulties (perhaps caused by learning disorders or ADD or pressure to get into a prestigious college). Maybe they feel socially awkward (perhaps from a lifetime of shyness), have lost a first love, are fighting an eating disorder, or are being harassed for being smart. Given the life and insecurities of teenagers, it would be safe to say that most teens lack emotional safety in some area. Sometimes the source of stress is obscure. Perhaps an individual's level of stress is no greater than that encountered by every teen, but he or she has fewer internal resources for coping with stress. A weak or poorly formed sense of identity, immature defenses against peer pressure, a compulsion to please others, and a thousand other psychological factors can contribute to adolescence being a time of danger and distress. It is not always easy to see which teens are experiencing this lack of safety most intensely or which ones lack the coping skills needed to deal with all the stresses they feel.

However, once teens begin repeating the mood swing produced by marijuana because life is less fun without it, they have embarked upon a high-risk course. They have begun to substitute a relatively dependable drug effect for doing the hard psychological work of developing internal means for dealing with life. From their standpoint, they wonder why they shouldn't solve their problems with pot, since it doesn't seem to be causing any problems. All their friends are smoking, or at least they are starting to be friends primarily with peers who *are* smoking (and often with a few older smokers, too, who may have more reliable access to a supply of marijuana). This is often a time of great enthusiasm for marijuana. Anything associated with the herb is seen in a positive light. Certain music finally makes sense and becomes a favorite. Life is good, or at least better than it was. Marijuana has given hope where before there was only stress.

Harmful Dependence on the Mood Swing

When *denial* takes over, the marijuana user enters a third stage on the path to addiction. This stage is characterized by an increasing involvement with fantasy and a decreasing involvement with the real world. Escape has become the primary motive for smoking pot. *Harmful* dependence results from the aftereffects of smoking (i.e., being dumbed down and burned out by a lasting reduction in the number of normal endocannabinoid receptor sites). Life without marijuana is now worse, more stressful, less enjoyable, and more problematic than before smoking started. Some of the problems created by neglecting responsibilities when stoned are waiting for the user every time he or she comes down. A gap develops between what many former peers are accomplishing and where the smoker's life has stalled. The discrepancy between being high and being straight is becoming more dramatic. Reality feels oppressive. Escape seems increasingly more necessary.

Irritability begins sneaking into the user's life. He or she feels increasingly impatient with straight life. Challenges are becoming more of an annoyance. Restrictions are seeming less reasonable. The sense of being trapped is mounting and freedom from arbitrary limits becomes more of a goal. Being stoned is the most appealing escape from life's burdens.

Using to Feel Normal

Addiction takes over as the *user (or stoner) identity becomes established.* At this point, teens are smoking to feel they can continue coping with life. They feel more normal when stoned. It has become difficult to function without pot. They may begin feeling the subtle physical withdrawal that consists of irritability, restlessness, sleep disturbance, labile emotions, and anxiety when they are not stoned. The only escape from this discomfort seems to be smoking marijuana again.

During this final stage, adolescents become more absorbed into the stoner lifestyle than ever before, but they may feel less excitement about smoking pot than earlier. Instead, there tends to be more hostility toward the straight world, more unquestioning acceptance of the value of pot, and a more sullen opposition to anything standing in the way of smoking. At times, the only acceptable state of mind becomes being high.

Robert Louis Stevenson described this final stage nicely in his book about Dr. Jekyll and Mr. Hyde. Whereas at first the good Dr. Jekyll became the libertine Mr. Hyde only when he ingested a powerful white powder, Mr. Hyde eventually took over spontaneously. At that point, the white powder was needed to get back to being Dr. Jekyll, back to feeling normal again. Every addict gets to this point. The alcohol field has the saying "First the man took the drink. Then the drink took the drink. And then the drink took the man." Addiction consumes and enslaves people, but their denial reasons that something (or more usually, someone) else is to blame. When our own denial accepts this reasoning, we are said to be "enabling" the continuation of someone's use.

Identifying the Signs of Addiction

If a teen is progressing toward addiction to marijuana, it is not necessary to wait until full-blown addiction exists to take action. Many parents agonize over their uncertainty of whether their children's deteriorating behavior and attitudes are truly due to using marijuana—if they really *are* smoking it—or if the behavior is just the normal process of growing up. The most important message here is that it doesn't matter. *It doesn't matter.* A parent's task is to set the expectations for the child's behavior. It is the child's task to meet these expectations. If a teen fails to meet these expectations, it becomes his or her task to prove to us that it is not because of using pot.

Following are the widely varying signs that teenagers provide when they are first seduced by marijuana, then devoted to it, and finally addicted.

Signs of Learning the Mood Swing

This is a tricky time. Since curiosity and a willingness to take risks are essentially healthy characteristics in adolescents, for most kids there is nothing necessarily pathologic about experimenting with marijuana. The vast majority of kids at this stage are not on their way toward addiction and will eventually self-regulate or stop their use. Their interest in learning what getting high on marijuana feels like is evidence only of normal curiosity. At this stage, kids are likely to show some *secretiveness*, although it may be no more intense than the secretiveness teens would show around sharing a *Playboy* magazine or unwrapping a condom for the first time. These are not experiences many teens want to share with their parents or to have their parents know about.

On the other hand, adolescents who *are* on their way toward addiction also pass through this first stage of learning the mood swing. For them, this is usually a very short stage, as they will most likely begin *seeking* the mood swing almost immediately—perhaps the next day. Occasionally I have heard teens relate that they were unable to get enough to smoke the very first time they experienced pot. Their friends were satisfied to play with the initial experiences of being high, while they wanted to get as high as possible. They loved "getting ripped and really messed up" right from the beginning. These teens were already running away from uncomfortable feelings, and the pot was just the latest, greatest distraction they had encountered.

I caution parents not to get upset at the initial interest their children may have about what drugs feel like. My thirteen-year-old daughter recently expressed curiosity about what being high on marijuana feels like. After experiencing years of drug prevention in her schools, seeing countless prevention videos, watching her older sister be placed in treatment for chemical dependence, knowing that her father is writing a book for Hazelden about marijuana, seeing actors using in movies, and listening to the buzz about smoking pot on the radio, in music, on TV, and among her friends—why wouldn't she wonder what all the fuss is about? Who wouldn't be curious? Of course she wonders.

The curiosity that brings our children to experiment with pot will most likely not bring them to ruin. When our children's curiosity is being piqued, we can take the opportunity to talk to them openly and not to respond with a knee-jerk catastrophizing reflex that will drive them away. Experimenting with marijuana does not make our children bad; it only places them at risk. We need to be available for our children when they are at risk.

Signs of Seeking the Mood Swing

A subtle change occurs as adolescents begin actively seeking the mood swing provided by marijuana. The change takes place on several levels simultaneously—inside the teens, between them and their friends, and in their interactions with their parents. Inside, they are turning toward a path that increasingly separates them from their parents. They begin feeling attracted to a new group of friends and may have less interest in old ones, though no reasons for this change may be evident. They may even be surprised that they have set out in this new direction, but smoking pot has an attraction that overrides their good judgment.

A new *defensiveness* begins to creep into the early smoker's behavior. In almost all cases, teens will feel ambivalent about the new choices they are making. At the same time, they will resist actually *feeling* this ambivalence. The defense people normally have against feeling any disapproval of themselves is to focus on the disapproval they see coming at them from the outside world. For teens, this means an intensification of conflict with their parents. Suddenly, they act as though their parents are criticizing them all the time. They become more defensive in general, which can be confusing to parents because neither child nor adult has a clear idea of the basis for the increasing combativeness.

Once teens have begun seeking the mood swing from pot, a new *manipulativeness* becomes necessary. It is no longer possible to let their parents know where they are every moment, whom they are with, or what they are doing. Parental supervision becomes a deterrent to smoking and is seen as the enemy. *Vague planning* becomes the routine, as they make it increasingly hard to nail down whose house they are going to, when the party ends, or whether they are going to the movies or somewhere else. They are frequently *unable to account for their time* when it takes them an hour and a half to walk distances that used to take half an hour. Or it becomes unclear whether they were at Joe's house from eight to ten and then at Bill's or whether they were at Bill's the whole time. And why was it exactly that they changed their plans and left Joe's early to get to Bill's? Hadn't plans been made to get to Bill's at ten because his parents weren't going to get home until then? Confusion, vagueness, and complexity become tools for achieving the privacy and secrecy needed to get high. Our teen begins attacking our efforts to keep track of his or her activities as being too controlling, too nosy, and untrusting. It is as though we are doing something wrong by pressing for more clarity regarding our child's comings and goings. We may be told to "loosen up" or "chill out." They may offer assurances about their safety and good behavior, sometimes with hostility, as though we are guilty of infantilizing them by being concerned. While most adolescents engage in some degree of manipulative behavior, teens in the early stages of being enthralled with pot will intensify their manipulativeness in concert with a whole pattern of other drug-focused behaviors.

Although many teens are introduced to pot by an old friend, *new friends* may come into their lives in ways that block any access to meeting them or to having contact with their parents. After all, how often are kids going to announce to their parents that they have met a neat new kid whom they want to have for an overnight when the main connection between them is that the new friend provides access to marijuana? Most new smokers gravitate into the orbit of their new using friends rather than the other way around. As a result, parents tend to learn only indirectly and piecemeal about these new friends. Nothing is straightforward when secretiveness is paramount.

Some kids begin playing with a new "in your face" *aggressiveness*. Grade-schoolers may decorate their room with marijuana-oriented posters and wear T-shirts with cannabis leaves and cartoon characters smoking joints. They seek out PG-13 and R-rated movies that casually glamorize smoking pot. And their curiosity exerts a gravitational pull toward older kids who are already in trouble. It doesn't take an addiction specialist to see that curiosity is running away with them. I have seen sixth graders manipulate their parents into feeling guilty for not letting them rent a Cheech and Chong movie that is entirely focused on smoking pot. *"All the other kids have seen it. Do you really think I'm going to start smoking pot just because I watch people in the movies do it? I know the difference between fantasy and reality. Don't you trust me? You are so controlling. No wonder I'd rather spend time at friends' homes. You don't let me have any fun. Any freedom. You are the worst, strictest, most uptight* [fill in whatever would be the most painful thing to hear, and they will probably say it eventually] *parents I know."*

Signs of Harmful Dependence on the Mood Swing

At this stage, a new personality starts moving into our child's body and slowly taking over. This is no longer the person we have known for the last twelve or fifteen years. *Erratic behavior* begins to make an appearance, as *swings in mood* become more intense. *School perform- ance worsens*, although there may be a flurry of reasons given for this. *"My teachers suck this year. Nothing they make us study is relevant to me. I don't need to go to college to do what I want to do."* As adolescents slip further into denial that their pot smoking is causing the very problems they are getting high to avoid, they *lose interest in the usual activities* that had previously filled their lives. Promising athletes no longer want to pursue their sport. Intelligent kids no longer strive to get good grades for the sheer pleasure of accomplishment. Strong readers lose interest in books.

Old friends who have not gone as far down the path of devoting themselves to marijuana *begin dropping away*, often inexplicably. Efforts to understand what happened to these relationships are treated as being intrusive. In fact, at this point any concern and love coming toward them from their parents becomes an irritant. The theme becomes *"Just leave me alone."* They make great efforts to distance themselves from parents. *Hostility* may become the norm in any interactions, as though even having a parent is an affront to their freedom. Some kids swing between accusing us of being the worst parents in the world one day and then returning to being comfortable in their old family role the next. Other kids have perfected sullenness as the only mood they permit themselves at home.

Part of what is occurring is that the teenagers are *changing their values to accommodate smoking pot.* On some level they know that skipping class to get high is wrong. On some level they know that sneaking out at night and lying about where they're going is wrong. On some level they know that our efforts to set some boundaries around their misbehavior is out of love and in their best interests, but they feel more irritation at this than anything else. They have gotten to the point of caring more about being able to continue smoking than about anything else. And so everything that interferes with smoking is either attacked or disregarded.

Signs of Using to Feel Normal

Severe emotional distress arrives on the scene at this point, unless *apathy* takes over. I have seen teens no longer care what happens to them, although there is usually such anger in the background that it is hard to believe they really "don't care." But the anger is ineffective. It is diffused and usually directed outward toward whatever they see as thwarting them—thwarting them from smoking as much as they want to, from being as happy as they think they would be if they were left alone, from having lives as easy as their delusions lead them to expect. *"I wish you would just get me an apartment and let me live alone! Then I'd be happy"* is the unrealistic refrain we hear in one form or another. Kids feel relieved of this distress when they are stoned again, and so the devotion to pot continues. In their minds, the rest of the world just doesn't understand them.

When not high on pot, *depression*, resulting from a chemically dulled brain and a deeply bored mind, can reach dangerous levels. One of the hallmarks of depression, when it fully takes over someone's life, is loss of perspective. Once this occurs, hope dissolves. It seems as though life has always been this way and always will be. There is no way out of the hole. Because adolescents are not known for how much perspective they have on their lives to begin with, they are easy victims for depression. Suicide can be very romanticized by teens. It can serve as the perfect way to express how wounded they feel by the world. And it certainly is an effective way to funnel hostility to forever wound parents—those who were supposed to love them into a successful life. As depression takes over, physical deterioration becomes more apparent, especially when the normal sleep/wake cycle is destroyed.

Possessing and smoking marijuana is currently illegal in the United States and is likely to remain illegal for minors no matter what laws adults make for themselves. As a result, heavy stoners regularly come to the attention of police and the juvenile justice system, and sometimes these consequences break through their denial. But because many addicted adolescents see nothing wrong with their marijuana use, contact with the legal system often further radicalizes them, adding to their *volatility and rage*. The arbitrariness of society's allowing alcohol, advertising alcohol, and making large profits from alcohol while prohibiting marijuana becomes a focal point for many people's anger. The willingness of a government to intrude on an individual's private subjective experience becomes something against which to wage righteous battle. Many pot smokers proudly become scofflaws and civil disobedients, bent on revealing society's hypocrisy and the government's disregard for individual rights. While these political arguments possess many legitimate points, teens who have personally become addicted to a drug that is harming them deeply undermine their stance. Rather than being able to channel their rage into an effective force for change, it too often runs them afoul with the law in ways that are mostly self-destructive.

Parental Signs: How Our Behavior Changes

It would be a mistake to think that all the signs of a child's increasing trouble with marijuana lie in his or her behavior. There are also many important signs that develop in the parents' behavior as well. The family as a whole usually begins to slide into some destructive patterns with the child's development of addiction. These signs are just as recognizable and important as anything that can be seen in a teen's life. It is also important for parents to look at themselves and their own behavior. They will often see several of the following signs.

Excessive Focus on the Using Child

It would be natural for concerned parents to begin focusing more time and energy on a child who is becoming addicted to marijuana, especially as school performance declines and the relationship with him or her turns negative. But this focus becomes problematic when a child's pot use becomes the central organizing principle for the family. I have seen families change their daily routines, to the detriment of other children in the family or to the detriment of the parents' relationship with each other, in an effort to control a child's smoking or rescue him or her from the natural consequences of marijuana use. When parents disrupt normal family activities to focus more on a child who is only trying to get more distant from them, resentments develop. For example, parents may routinely begin skipping one child's baseball games because they are reluctant to leave another child home alone, for fear he or she will get stoned. When the family's health as a whole is being sacrificed in unsuccessful efforts to corral a teen who has become harmfully involved with marijuana, this becomes a sign in and of itself of the degree of trouble that has developed.

Scapegoating the Using Child

At some point parents often start blaming the "problem" child for everything that is going wrong with the family. The child in trouble begins being blamed for causing tension between spouses. If only he or she would start behaving, the family would return to being a safe haven for everyone. Having a scapegoat removes the need for parents to look at their own behavior. The scapegoat, as parents see it, *makes* their blood boil. The scapegoat *makes* them yell. The scapegoat *makes* them more rigid and controlling. The scapegoat *makes* them argue with each other. The scapegoat *makes* them act crazy and want to strike out at them, verbally and even physically.

Once teens take on the role of scapegoat, they may feel they are getting blamed for things they haven't even done. They may conclude that if they are suffering the punishments, they might as well commit the crime. Anger at being blamed for everything that goes wrong in the family often contributes to further misbehavior, and they are soon earning the reputation they have been given. A terrible barrage of judgment and blaming can be poured onto the scapegoat out of frustration, anger, and impotence. Whether scapegoated teens show it or not, they will absorb this blame and begin developing a deep sense of inadequacy and shame to match its intensity. Scapegoating destroys families, and does more to hide the underlying truth than to reveal it.

Scapegoating also obscures the parents' vision of what changes they might need to make themselves. As poorly as their child may be behaving, most parents also have their own work to do, their own development to foster, in order to maintain their integrity and values through a stressful time. Scapegoating a child takes the focus off the ways parents might be making a bad situation worse. It releases parents from having to take a hard look at themselves. As justified as scapegoating might feel to a harried parent, it too conveniently lets parents off the hook, keeping them from examining their own behavior and their often well-meaning, but ineffectual, motivations.

Increasing Efforts to Control

Parents have a wide variety of reactions to watching their teen begin spinning out of control. Fear is palpable for most. Some respond to this fear by throwing up their hands and saying, *"What can I do? He's out of control"* or *"She's got a right to make her own choices,"* but then interfering with any consequences in an attempt to protect their child. Others are paralyzed into inaction by the fear, wanting desperately to help but ashamed to let others know what may be happening to their family. They shake inside and hope for the best. Perhaps the most common response, however, is to get into action, to begin going to the mat, fighting to reestablish control, not letting their kid push them around. *"I'll make him mind, by God!"*

On one level, trying to control a teenager by force and willpower feels good. I remember feeling that my role as a father meant being willing to do battle with any intruder into my home, including pot. If marijuana was going to be brought into my child's bedroom, I was going to ferret it out. If she was going to lock her bedroom door, I was going to remove the whole doorknob. If she was going to sneak out after going to bed, I was going to be waiting out in the yard to head her off at the pass. I was in action!

Some of the steps I took were useful, but the energy underlying my "doing battle" with my daughter was misguided. The more parents try to forcibly control their child's behavior, the more their child's self-esteem depends on resisting the coercion. I was adding fuel to the fire between us. If she was blaming me for how miserable she felt, my threats and efforts to bully her into abstinence were giving her proof that I really was overbearing. In a very real sense, I was trying to take the choices she was making away from her instead of making sure that the consequences for those choices were clear and undesirable. I was inadvertently turning the battle over whether or not to smoke, which rightfully existed wholly within her, into a battle between herself and me. That is a battle that can never be won.

Volatile Arguments

As matters deteriorate and everyone's misery deepens, repetitive arguments often take on a familiar and more volatile pattern. A teen who bounces back and forth every day between being stoned and withdrawing develops labile emotions. The parents' emotions, strained by fear and a sense of failure, have reached the trigger point. Insults become more vile. Language descends to the gutter. Everyone is trying desperately to be listened to. And everyone is further inflamed by what the other says. Physical violence may be threatened or may actually erupt as people are looking for some way to get through to the other.

At this point, few people are stopping long enough to look at how out of line their own behavior has gotten. Instead, they automatically blame the other's outrageous behavior for causing their own excesses.

Splitting the Parents

Having two parents is a tremendous advantage in dealing with any adolescent, except when the two are having difficulty being in agreement. At times parents can feel more frustration and get into more heated arguments with each other than with the child who is in trouble. As tensions rise and fear that a child is in harm's way mounts, the need to be doing the "right thing" becomes more urgent. Often one parent is ready to pull the trigger on an important consequence (e.g., taking the child for professional evaluation or placing him or her in a treatment program), but the other feels the spouse is overreacting. One parent often breaks through denial first, while the other is still trying to believe their child is only going through a phase. One thinks they have to love their child enough to win him or her back, while the other argues for a firmer stance. The conflict between parents can be futile, wrenching, and even damaging if they are not careful. In instances where one parent is also concerned about the other parent's abuse of alcohol or other drugs, the complexities facing them as a couple increase exponentially. It is often not only the adolescent who is in crisis, but the family as a whole and the marriage itself.

Of course, teens are also experts at intensifying the split between their parents. If the father puffs himself up and becomes more stern and controlling, the child may seek warm reassurances from the mother. If the mother screams at her child for "going to hell in a handbasket," the kid may give a knowing glance to Dad, trying to recruit him into an alliance around how "hysterical" Mom can be. Teens are experts at dividing parents to nullify their effectiveness.

Parents are wise not to waste time scapegoating a child for the splitting he or she is trying to create. The child is desperate and simply doing what works. The parents' task is to stop letting it work. When parents see a rift opening between them, it is often a sign that their child is in trouble with marijuana.

Parental Sense of Failure and Guilt

There seems to be no end to the self-recrimination that many of us feel when watching our son or daughter become dependent on marijuana. *"Where did I go wrong as a parent? Was I too lenient? Too strict? Too blind or too intrusive? How did I fail to see what was happening soon enough to stop it?"*

Self-blame is based on the same mistaken beliefs that lead us to think we can *make* our kids behave if we only try hard enough or find the right strategy. The illusion we maintain is that we have control over our children's fates, over their desires and choices, over the very direction of their lives. When we "fail" to control their lives enough to guarantee a successful outcome, we blame ourselves. But the reality is that *we* are not at the center of our children's lives; *they* are at the center of their own lives. We model life for our children and then *they* make whatever choices they are going to make. If we have done our best to love and guide them well, despite our many flaws and inadequacies, then they are the authors of their own misery. They have made poor choices, despite having been given more than enough information and encouragement to use better judgment. It is not our fault that they are suffering the natural consequences of those poor choices. It is our job only to help them understand the real source of their pain and to give them the resources and encouragement to begin making better, healthier choices.

Each child brings something new, something entirely his or her own, into the world. We have no control over who our children ultimately are. We can take no final credit and we deserve no final blame for how they live their lives, only how we live our own. When we begin sliding into a pit of guilt and failure because one of our children has fallen into addiction, it is often a sign that we have bought into the child's distorted view that we are to blame for his or her misery.

Support for Parents

If we are wondering whether our child is getting into trouble with marijuana, we need to *listen to our intuition*. The feeling of distress in our gut is almost certainly there for a reason, although marijuana is only one possibility.

There are many things we can do to check out our intuition. Start going to Al-Anon and talking about what we fear. Al-Anon is an antidote for this fear. The support organization for spouses of alcoholics that grew up alongside Alcoholic Anonymous has been helping people for decades to live with the simple truth that "you can lead a horse to water, but you can't make it drink." It is as literally and physically impossible to force a horse to drink as it is to control the weather. In a similar vein, it is impossible to force anyone to value sobriety. To use the language of Al-Anon, we are powerless to make choices for others. Our kids are free to want what they choose to want, and we have no responsibility for their desires.

Acknowledging our powerlessness to make the horse drink restores us to a more sane perspective and permits us to try more effective approaches. For example, moving the watering trough away from an electric fence to make it more attractive and keeping the horse trotting so it builds up a thirst increases the likelihood that it will eventually choose to take a drink. By not wasting energy trying to control things that are outside our control (such as the horse's mind), we can focus on changing what is under our control. Similarly, Al-Anon helps us stop trying to control the decisions people in trouble with drugs make. Instead, we can do what is possible to make recovery look more attractive, while also making continued use of pot more uncomfortable. In most cases, all we have to do is to stop protecting a drug abuser from the natural consequences of his or her own behavior. Al-Anon's approach shows more respect to an addict by no longer trying to wrest control of the addict's life from him or her, but rather acknowledging his or her inherent freedom. As counterintuitive as accepting our powerlessness to make a child behave may seem, it is the healthiest attitude for approaching any child who has gotten into trouble with marijuana.

Implementing this new approach is not easy. It requires letting go of the tight grasp we have been trying to keep on our child. The analogy that works for many parents is that of being in an airplane when the oxygen masks drop down. Taking care to be sure our oxygen supply is secured first before trying to put the mask on our child is recommended. We will be no help to anyone if we let ourselves expire while trying to save someone else. Most of us will need a lot of support from others who have already been down the same path if we are to be able to rethink, and refeel, the relationship with a child who is in trouble and to put our own self-care first when necessary.

It is important to talk to our child about our concerns. But it is just as important to talk to other parents, especially parents who have eventually seen their child enter recovery. We need to talk to them about what we've intuited, as well as about all the signs in our child's behavior—the defensiveness, secretiveness, vagueness, new friends, loss of normal interests, decline in school performance, erratic behavior, more volatile emotions or apathy, hostility, loss of old friends, serious depression, or legal troubles. At the same time, we must keep an eye on our own behavior and that of the family as a whole. If we find the courage to talk to other parents about how we have begun focusing all our attention on the child we are concerned about, scapegoating him or her, increasing our efforts to control him or her, getting angrier and into progressively more volatile arguments, feeling more conflict with our spouse or more guilty and inadequate, we will almost certainly find the support needed to continue facing the crisis in our family.

In the end, there are usually far more signs of developing trouble than we were first aware of. Only with time do they become clear. However, as soon as we have gone on the lookout for whatever signs we can find, it is already time to seek consultation with a professional familiar with the ins and outs of adolescent addiction. We need to get help. That is, after all, what we hope our child will do.

Chapter 7

Talking to Teens about Your Use:
For Those Who *Have* Inhaled

I had the opportunity this past year to participate in a family therapy session conducted by a man skilled in the growing field of equine therapy—the art of working with horses to teach people basic truths about relationships. What unfolded illustrated the critical role that integrity plays in a successful relationship between parent and child.

A Lesson in Integrity

The therapist placed a parent in the middle of a round horse pen. He told him to trace a circle in the dust ten feet in diameter around himself. Then he led a friendly horse into the pen and let it loose. The horse immediately walked up to the man in the middle of the pen and began nuzzling him. "Without touching the horse I want you to get it to stay out of your circle," the therapist instructed. Getting a twelve-hundred-pound animal to do voluntarily what he wanted it to do seemed as formidable as getting a hostile teenager to clean up his or her room.

The man stood dumbfounded, paralyzed by the lack of power he felt. The horse nudged him from behind with its muzzle and knocked the man forward. He turned and waved his arms in an attempt to get the horse to back up. Instead it just turned its head and looked away, ignoring the man's efforts. He clucked and told the horse to move. It rubbed the side of its head against the man's shoulder. "How can I get something to move that's so much bigger than me?" the man asked in defeat.

"Not by talking to me," the therapist replied. "I think it likes you. I think you're going to have to convince it you mean business."

The man spread his feet a bit and put on his sternest, bravest expression. "Move, get out of here," he shouted at the horse, to no avail. It looked away again, but did not move. "It's not going to move if it doesn't want to, and I can't make it," the man tried to explain.

The therapist invited the man's wife to take his place. As soon as the horse nestled up to her, she turned toward it abruptly, slapped her thigh loudly, and waved her other hand in the horse's face. The horse was startled. She stepped toward it, into the horse's space, and shouted at it to move. To her husband's surprise, the horse jumped back and began trotting warily around the perimeter of the pen.

"Why did that work?" her husband asked.

"Tell him what you did," the therapist coaxed her.

"It's not what I *did*," she explained. "I didn't really know what I was going to do. But I sure as hell was going to do whatever it took to get that damn animal out of my space."

"You see?" the therapist pointed out. "Horses are perfectly tuned into our intention. You can't pretend you're going to make the horse move. You have to really mean it and really believe it. You cannot lie to a horse. Integrity is everything. Everything."

One of the fundamental characteristics of horses is that they are prey, not predators. As prey, they must continually assess surrounding dangers. A passing wolf that has just eaten is nothing to fear. A hungry one must be responded to immediately. Our children are at least as aware and intelligent, emotionally, as horses. This may be especially true during the teen years when they feel beleaguered by a world that is increasingly expecting things from them. Teens, who also often feel like prey, will sense almost unerringly whether we approach them with hidden agendas or with integrity.

Assessing Your Relationship with Drugs and Alcohol, Past and Present

Integrity begins inside, with an honest assessment of ourselves. There is no doubt that most adults with a history of smoking marijuana had a lot of fun. So much so that few have accurately assessed the risks they took by their behavior. Before deciding how, or if, to talk to our children about our marijuana use, we are wise to consider just how healthy our relationship has been with the drugs we have known.

As mentioned in chapter 3, I find the criteria developed by Andrew Weil for assessing the health of one's relationship with any drug to be helpful. Following are four signs of an unhealthy relationship with any drug:

- ignorance that the substance is a drug and of what it does to the body
- loss of the desired effect with increasing frequency of use
- difficulty separating from the drug
- impairment of health or social functioning

When looking at our own experiences with marijuana (or alcohol and any other mood-altering drugs we have experienced, including prescription medications), we need to ask ourselves whether we were truly aware that the chemical we were using is a drug and of what it was doing to our brains. Most of us were too intent on defending our marijuana use to be willing to think of it as a drug. Like kids, and many adults today, we generally passed it off as a natural plant, an herb. Few of us took heed of warnings that it might have a negative impact on our brains or our lives, discounting this as hysterical lies by the older generation. We were comfortable propagating the myth of "natural means safe." And few of us were willing to admit that it had any possibility of being addictive. Most of us, in fact, had little idea of what addiction actually means.

Were our early experiences with marijuana positive enough that we got into a pattern of chasing after the high during our adult years, hoping that pot could again have that same fresh, new feeling we remember? Most people eventually have to admit that nothing new is happening when they smoke. Whereas they initially felt that smoking opened up new perspectives on the world, they are now just repeating the same experience. The drug eventually provides only an approximation of the initial experience, really. Repeating the approximation is no longer drug experimentation. It has become a process of seeking the old mood swing, often as a distraction from the rest of life.

Did we ever tell ourselves that it was time to stop smoking before we actually did stop? *If* we stopped. Did we have difficulty replacing the time spent getting high with other things that brought as much pleasure? Do we still miss getting stoned? Many people have difficulty being honest about whether they have experienced trouble separating from marijuana. This does not necessarily mean that they have experienced withdrawal symptoms, which are not a prominent phenomenon with marijuana. It simply means that at some point in life it was more desirable, or easier, to get stoned than to find healthier, more creative ways to use the weekend. Difficulty separating from pot means that it has become a pattern, a habit that has woven its way into the fabric of life, maybe into the fabric of one's personality. Pulling this thread out of life's fabric usually requires some real work.

Did we ever worry about what we were doing to our lungs when we were smoking? Have we wondered whether we still live with an increased risk for cancer? Marijuana smoke contains the same chemicals known to be toxic to the lungs as tobacco smoke. I have known athletes as young as thirteen years old who were smoking pot frequently enough that their stamina on the soccer field was impaired. They had chest pains when they tried to go all out for a whole practice.

Are there people who distanced themselves from us because they were not interested in joining a circle of friends that included pot? Did old friends drift away as they got married, stopped smoking, moved on while we continued to get high? Have we lied to friends or family to cover up our smoking? (Have we lied to ourselves?) Did we do a notch less well in school than we would have without marijuana as our companion? Have we been less assertive at work, less aggressive, less sharp, less competent, less willing or interested in taking on new levels of responsibility? It is hard to calculate the effect of missed opportunities, especially when they slip past us in subtle, unnoticed ways. I have known people who chose jobs, such as sales positions, that provided great freedom out in the field, largely because the lack of supervision enabled them to continue smoking pot throughout the day.

Do we feel that our authority with our children is compromised because of our relationship to marijuana (alcohol or other drugs)? Do we lie to our children when they smell smoke on our breath or clothes, saying that we occasionally sneak a cigarette when we were actually getting stoned out in the garage? Has our use of marijuana compromised our integrity?

Alcoholics Anonymous encourages its members to evaluate their relationship to drugs with "rigorous honesty," taking inventory not only of the fun but also of the fear; not only of the excitement, but also of the risks. Only then will we be in a position to speak with integrity to our children. Only then will our words hold any substance and meaning for them. If it is our expectation that they will speak to us with honesty, we must approach them with no less.

What to Tell the Kids about Our Use

It's no secret that children learn more from what we do than from what we say. This helps explain why alcohol and drug prevention pro-grams become progressively less effective with older children. Once youngsters begin to see the discrepancies between what society is try-ing to inculcate in them and how adults actually behave, they feel justified in rejecting the information. Again, integrity is critical.

Deciding how much to reveal to a child requires a good sense of that child's level of maturity. We must match the information we give to their capacity to understand. As a result of these limitations, speak-ing honestly to a child rarely means full disclosure. Speaking to our children about our marijuana use is a lot like talking to them about sex. We want to be honest and to tell the truth, within their limits to understand and integrate what they are hearing. We can still be in integrity when withholding information that a child is not yet ready to understand or when drawing a boundary around what is too private to reveal comfortably or with benefit to anyone.

The process of speaking to a child about our marijuana history is also quite different depending on whether we're still smoking pot. The difference is great enough that I will address each situation separately.

If You Used in the Past

Most parents who experimented with pot in the sixties, seventies, or eighties no longer smoke today. According to the 2000 *National House-hold Survey on Drug Abuse* conducted by the Substance Abuse and Mental Health Services Administration (SAMHSA), the peak age for having smoked during the previous month was eighteen. Among twenty-five-year-olds, only 8 percent had smoked during the previous month, and only 1 percent of fifty-year-olds had. Thirty-two years earlier, when those fifty-year-olds were high school seniors, 40 percent of teens in that age group had reported trying marijuana. How important is it for them to tell their children about their use? Can't such honesty backfire by giv-ing kids permission to experiment, too? Isn't discretion sometimes called for more than honesty? Two important points are helpful in considering if and when to talk to your kids about your past experience with marijuana. The first is the age of onset and the second is risk assessment.

Age of Onset

There is a world of difference between first experimenting with marijuana at twelve years old and first experimenting with it at twenty years old. Many adults miss this distinction. As a result, parents who first smoked pot at twenty often tend to "excuse" a ninth grader's experimenting with it because they understand the attraction. What they fail to take into account is the immense difference in psychological development between these two ages.

If we want our twelve- or fourteen-year-old child to avoid or delay smoking marijuana, we do not have to volunteer that we smoked it in college. It is highly unlikely that a child this young would be able to understand the real significance of this age difference. Children see the world through the lens of their current age and do not truly understand what it means to be of college age.

Sometimes, however, we may be asked directly whether we have smoked pot. What to do then? First, know that this might be like the "Where do babies come from?" question. Jumping into details about intercourse may miss the point when "Mommies usually have them in the hospital" may be all our child wants to know. We can start by finding a place of genuine curiosity within ourselves and ask why he or she wants to know. Frequently, children announce their desire to talk about themselves by first asking a question. Depending on their age, a child might answer, "My friend said people who smoke marijuana even once usually get lung cancer and Uncle Joe died of lung cancer." In this case, the question was not really about marijuana as much as it was about concern for a parent's health. Or a child might answer, "My teacher said everyone tried marijuana back in the sixties." In this case, the parent has an opportunity to correct a misperception before waiting to see if the child is going to pursue knowing about the parent's personal history. Or an older child could answer, "Well, some of my friends have started smoking it. So, you know, I've had a few opportunities, and . . ." In this case, the parent really is being asked to share past experiences with a child who is open to being given some guidelines to help in making the choices that he or she is facing.

When pressed to provide a direct answer to a direct question, parents have found several ways to respond. We might say something like "Certainly not at your age." A child may persist, "Well, when did you first smoke pot?" At that point we may decide it is appropriate to reveal more information. Some parents choose to say, "When you get to be the age that I first tried marijuana, I'll tell you. But that's not going to be for a long time." Others will give a direct answer, but it is rarely enough to simply give the age we first tried pot. The timing is right for a more in-depth discussion about the topic. One indication that it is safe to be honest about our history is that our child is available and open to real dialogue. Otherwise, he or she may simply be fishing for another justification for his or her own use. For those parents who *did* start smoking marijuana at twelve or fourteen, the following section becomes particularly relevant.

Assessing Risk Accurately

There is probably no reason to hesitate in telling a child about our marijuana experiences if we started smoking at thirteen, quickly got addicted, failed our freshman year of high school, got arrested, and were sent to a treatment center by the time we were sixteen. To keep this cautionary tale hidden, perhaps out of embarrassment, deprives the next generation of valuable information about hereditary risk for addiction.

The majority of parents with a history of marijuana use, however, did not experience disaster. In fact, the core of the dilemma facing most parents is that they think, "*I did it, and I turned out okay. How can I tell my children it will be different for them?*" To many parents, the fact that smoking pot never amounted to anything more important than having a good time years ago greatly complicates the fear they now feel for their children. Where do integrity and honesty lie now? Do parents say, "I had a great time with pot; just be careful"? Or do they try to justify their fears by stressing the danger of today's stronger pot?

I think the answer for parents lies in three approaches. First, after acknowledging former pot use, they also acknowledge their legitimate concern for their child's health and safety. Second, they focus attention on the profound differences inherent in smoking pot at an age younger than when they smoked (if that is true). Third, they are prepared to discuss realistically the risks they took with marijuana when they were younger.

Euphoric recall often interferes with our memory of drug experiences. We remember the most intense portions of the experience, which were often the excitement and fun, while forgetting the downside. Euphoric recall of smoking days often keeps people from honestly assessing the risks they courted and the prices they may have paid. Mostly, people remember the fun times—the rock concerts, the trips to the ice-cream store when the munchies took over, and watching the *Rocky Horror Picture Show* in a theater full of other stoners. What they tend to forget is that they took the risk (to themselves and others) of driving to the concerts while high. Or they forget the time they had to eat a joint to keep from being arrested by police who stopped them for jaywalking, or the time they let friends talk them out of studying for a test so they could get high all weekend. They forget about all the smoke they sucked into their lungs for years and about getting so high that they became too sexual with a good friend's date and lost the friendship. They may have even forgotten the anxiety they started to feel whenever they smoked (pot smokers may eventually experience anxiety and panic attacks) or the number of times they decided not to smoke anymore, only to go back on that promise to themselves the first time they were tempted. And they still may not understand how their marijuana use may have delayed developing adult coping skills and a stable sense of identity.

Simply put, few adults had a realistic assessment of the risks, legal and psychological, that they were taking while using marijuana in their youth. If we are going to talk to our children about those times, it is helpful to reassess them first, this time from an adult and more informed perspective.

If You're Using Now

Parents who routinely relax and calm their stress and anxieties with a daily drink or two, or with a joint, diminish their authority to encourage teenage children to abstain from using drugs or alcohol. Some adults who continue to smoke pot understand this discrepancy and refrain from trying to influence their children, permitting them to make their own choices about marijuana. This solves the dilemma, but probably not in the most helpful way. The civil libertarian approach of "live and let live" and the Zen philosophy that "everyone must find his or her own path" may work well for adults, but these approaches permit adolescents to drift aimlessly when what they may need is strong values and boundaries. Leaving teens without guidance when our behavior is modeling a lifestyle that may be harmful to them disregards an essential responsibility of parenting.

Those of us who continue to use marijuana can commit ourselves to three things that will be helpful to our children. The first is honesty. We need to assess accurately our history of marijuana use and be willing to apply this honesty to the present as well. Whether we are parents, educators, counselors, or police, when we discuss with kids the reasons people are attracted to marijuana and how it may affect them, we must have enough integrity to be asking the same uncomfortable questions of ourselves if we are going to have any credibility. Being a parent can be very demanding. It creates a responsibility to live more publicly than if no children were looking at our behavior for examples to follow or reject. The first commitment to our children's and our health is to make an ongoing, rigorously honest assessment of the risks in continuing our marijuana use.

The second commitment, if smoking marijuana continues to be part of our lives, is to *talk* to our children, especially if we openly smoke in front of them. If a child knows we are smoking, it is important not to deny this reality, either directly or by pretense. We may fool our children for a while, but they are almost certainly going to discover the truth eventually. When that happens, we are likely to lose all credibility and trust, and not only about pot.

We can talk to our children in terms that are appropriate to how they comprehend the world in general, the same way someone who regularly drinks wine at dinner would naturally discuss this behavior from time to time. If we believe marijuana plays the same beneficial lifestyle role that nightly wine plays for others, then we need to be open with our children about this belief. But we also need to clearly indicate at what age we believe this lifestyle becomes safe and appropriate for someone, just as a responsible wine drinker would. And we need to be clear that marijuana remains illegal, which brings risks that cannot be ignored.

The third commitment those of us who continue to smoke marijuana can make that would be helpful to our children is *to be willing to abstain* at whatever point this would be helpful to any family member having trouble controlling marijuana use. This commitment acknowledges that, while we may be using pot without any apparent negative effects, we understand that this may not be possible for everyone. If our child falls into the minority of adolescents who become harmfully involved with pot, we need to stop bringing weed into his or her world. If we are unwilling to make this commitment, it may be evidence that we have developed significant difficulty separating from the drug and that our relationship with pot is less healthy than we want to believe. This takes us back to the first commitment: an ongoing assessment of the risks being taken by smoking.

Wearing the Mantle of Authority

The question of whether to talk to our children about our own history of marijuana use taps into one of the central difficulties the current generation of parents experiences with our role—our own discomfort with authority. The decade of the sixties reignited the American tradition of not trusting authority and ushered in new degrees of freedom for many people. But it also complicated our ability to wear the mantle of authority once it came time for this responsibility to be accepted. The discomfort with now *being* an authority plays itself out in home after home, family after family, throughout our nation's communities, in an ineffective style of parenting. Too often, we justify overlooking our children's mistakes by remembering our own. The fact that many of us smoked marijuana does not mean that we don't have the right or responsibility to provide the best possible advice to the children of today.

This chapter is an invitation to wrestle with the truth about our relationship to marijuana, alcohol, and other drugs (including mind-altering prescription drugs such as Valium, Xanax, sleeping pills, and pain medications). The honesty we achieve here creates the integrity we need in order to be helpful to our children. But integrity is not all that is needed. Most of us also have to wrestle with what it means to assert parental authority. Once we have children of our own, we need to question whether we can maintain the same simplistic, black-and-white attitude about parental authority that many of us developed during our adolescence. As parents, we're required to reach another level of maturation.

The following chapter turns to the question of what authority we are willing, and able, to assert in the protection of our child's health and safety.

Chapter 8

Intervening to Protect a Child: Exercising Parental Authority

This chapter addresses the minority of teens who experience the majority of damage from pot. How should parents respond once they believe that their child, their brother's or sister's child, or a good friend's teen is in trouble with marijuana?

An addicted person's entire endocannabinoid system is chronically out of balance, which throws many of the brain's other chemicals out of whack as well. At this point, thinking is no longer clear and judgment is impaired. Addicts lose control of their drug use without understanding the true gravity of the situation. As a result, addicted adolescents often think parents (and teachers) are the cause of whatever problems they have. Their circle of using friends often reinforces this misconception.

In outlining options available for intervening in a teen's addiction, I assume that many parents are at first uncomfortable with direct intervention. Just at the point in life when we generally want to allow our children more freedom, intervention seems to call on us to reverse direction. So it's important to keep a few points in mind. Addicted teens begin acting less and less like responsible adults as the drug gradually takes over. Rather than maturing, their psychological growth stalls or may even slip backward. While their bodies may be growing, their capacity to take good care of themselves in the real world is shrinking. Providing more freedom makes no sense when they are hurting themselves and others with the license they are already taking. They are still under eighteen, they are still legally under parental control, and, if we do not act to protect their health and safety, who will?

As repugnant as it may be for many of us to restrict an adolescent's freedom, we can consider the precedent set for this by the medical field. When the public's health is at stake, civil liberties take a back seat to good public health policies. People with infectious diseases are sometimes quarantined, even against their will. Public health takes precedence over individual rights when the protection of those rights endangers the patient and others. The greater good requires the long view. In the case of an addicted teen, it is the individual and his or her family who are most directly put at risk, but the community as a whole is also affected negatively. Freedom must sometimes be temporarily curtailed to protect health for the long run.

Our capacity to fulfill the role of a parent is tested by adolescence itself, but an addicted adolescent can be the supreme test. We need support to respond sanely and effectively. Timing is also important. The sooner we take an active role in altering the course of our child's life, the more influence our actions will have on the child's future. But how should we respond? What control is really possible over anyone? How do we avoid escalating the hatred our child may already feel for us? How do we avoid getting into a greater power struggle with a child who is already in full rebellion?

Preparing for Intervention

We need to stop a moment and take a deep breath. We have some preparation to do first, before acting. No one gets helped if we go crazy with our own anxiety. No one benefits if we go ballistic out of our own frustration and anger. Remember that the goal is to protect the child's health and safety. Keeping an eye on that basic goal will help as we prepare to take some actions that may at times be hard for us.

Two critical steps in first responding effectively to the family's crisis are (1) finding support for ourselves and (2) understanding the limit of what lies under our control. Fortunately, we can approach these important issues simultaneously.

Chapter 6 introduced the dilemma we face regarding our limited ability to control a teenager's behavior, much like the problem of how to get a horse to *want* to take a drink of water. The most natural and logical response our minds come up with when faced with a teenager's difficult behavior is to clamp down harder, to impose control from the outside. There is a paradox here, however, that must eventually be confronted. We can go to extraordinary lengths to stop teens from using marijuana. We can force them to change schools. We can never let them out of our sight. We can ground them for all eternity. We can bolt their windows shut. Of course, we will have to sacrifice our entire life to clamp down this hard. We will probably have to quit our job, abandon caring for our other children, get almost no sleep, and maintain a vigilance that quickly leads to total exhaustion. Despite all this, we will not be able to *make* our children stop wanting to smoke pot. No matter how strongly we may will it, we can't control another's mind.

Short of brainwashing someone, we are unable to get into other people's heads and control what they think, what they want, or how they feel. We are powerless over any addict's mind. We cannot successfully force someone to change his or her mind, to see things more clearly, or to be willing to do what we think is in his or her best interests. In reality, adolescents are absolutely free to find and smoke pot if they want to. The wisdom of Al-Anon encourages us to stop wasting energy trying to control the things that the universe never gives us any means to control and to concentrate instead on what realistically does lie within our powers.

We *can* control our own behavior. We *can* refrain from saying things that are guaranteed to inflame what is already a bad situation. We *can* stop reacting out of anger and hatred. We *can* stop trying to control the addict by shaming him or her. We *can* stop standing in the way of the consequences that our children will naturally experience as a result of their addiction. Getting out of the way means no longer rescuing them in the thousand ways we do—out of our concern, out of our love, and out of our desire to prevent them from as much pain as we can. It may mean no longer hiding their marijuana use from other family members, from neighbors, from teachers and the principal, or even from the police. Many parents steadfastly refuse to permit a child to sneak marijuana into the home and endanger younger brothers and sisters. When they find evidence that this rule has been broken after fully warning their child, they call the police for assistance. While we do not have control over our children's choices, we do have control over whether we continue shielding them from the natural consequences. Being held accountable is not the worst thing that can happen to a teen.

Al-Anon

It is not easy to hold back an angry tongue or to avoid being consumed by resentments when living with a child who has become dependent on marijuana. It takes a community to support us during these trying times. It also takes a community to keep enough hope alive to take the courageous stands needed to stop protecting our children from their own choices. The community waiting to help can be found at Al-Anon meetings. Gathered at these meetings are people who have grown wise from facing the trials of living with an addict.

Al-Anon had its beginning soon after Alcoholics Anonymous was born. Initially made up of the wives of alcoholics who were getting sober through AA, members of the Al-Anon Family Groups discovered that they were also greatly helped by applying the Twelve Step program developed by AA to their own lives. Al-Anon groups exist in nearly every community today and are attended by wives, husbands, brothers, sisters, children, and parents of alcoholics and addicts. Many communities have Al-Anon meetings with a special focus on parents. Anyone who finds that his or her own behavior and self-esteem are whirling out of control as a result of being in a close relationship with someone who is chemically dependent will find that Al-Anon can help in regaining peace of mind.

Al-Anon usually lists its phone number in the Yellow Pages under "Alcoholism"; a quick call is all that is needed to have a list of local meetings mailed to you. No formal membership or dues are required. Meetings last about an hour and usually start with a member sharing his or her story or readings from Al-Anon literature followed by voluntary sharing by those in attendance. Newcomers are always welcomed but should feel no need to speak if they wish to remain silent. Attendees remain anonymous to each other, and whatever is said in meetings is held in strict confidence.

People have many reasons for refusing to take advantage of the support offered by a Twelve Step group such as Al-Anon. They may already feel so beleaguered that adding another time-consuming activity only stresses them further, especially if it takes away from time spent at home with family. Many people do not understand the intent of Al-Anon, believing that its primary purpose is to provide a place to complain about addicts. The idea of talking about personal problems, even within an anonymous environment, is difficult for people who are still trying to keep others outside the family from seeing their dirty laundry. They may think they ought to be able to solve their family's problems on their own, or they are afraid to acknowledge the true depth of their pain and despair, trying to control it by hiding it from themselves and others. All of these are normal responses to finding ourselves in an undesirable situation we didn't cause and haven't been able to control. The sooner we break through our own denial, the sooner we can help our children break through their denial. Staying isolated keeps us from learning that pain shared is pain lightened.

The bottom line is simple, really. Parents are telling (or maybe yelling at) their child that there is a better way and people can help him or her find it. But the child remains maddeningly deaf. At the same time, Al-Anon is offering parents a better way to deal with a family member's addiction and providing access to people in the community who can help. Parents who resist getting help for themselves compromise their authority when insisting that their child accept help. It is a matter of integrity.

Al-Anon calls upon people to detach from the addict in their lives. To most parents, this sounds both absurd and impossible at first. Then it may sound just plain wrong. How can we no longer *care* what happens to our own flesh and blood? Over time, however, through listening to longtime Al-Anon attendees share their experiences, successes, and hopes for the future, people gradually come to understand that detachment does not mean "not caring." Al-Anon members care very deeply about friends and relatives who are chemically dependent but have learned to detach their own self-esteem and happiness from the unreliable behavior of alcoholics and addicts. Detaching enables them to achieve greater well-being personally, while paradoxically freeing the addict from useless power struggles with them.

By detaching from a teen who has become harmfully involved with marijuana, parents become free to care more deeply about their child rather than being consumed with anger and resentment. Detaching also does not mean disconnecting from a child. With detachment, parents become free to have real empathy for the misery their child is feeling as he or she is lost in addiction. Nor does detaching mean that parents no longer hold a child responsible for his or her behavior. Detaching means that parents no longer have to be the judge, jury, and executioner for every mistake their child makes. We can trust that permitting the natural consequences to flow has the greatest likelihood of waking our child up to the reality of his or her addiction.

Detaching begins with recognizing that a child is in the clutches of a disease—the disease called addiction. His or her brain is compromised. The drug addiction is not revealing who the child truly is but rather is concealing his or her true self underneath a thick layer of denial and distorted behavior. As detachment deepens, parents stop thinking of the disease afflicting a child as a source of personal shame. In many ways, the addiction that has overtaken a child has nothing to do with his or her parents. The symptoms of addiction resemble those of diabetes more than they resemble a moral lapse or willful misbehavior. Detachment means that parents' self-esteem no longer rests on their child's behavior; it rests predominately on their own behavior. Have *they*, as parents, broken their denial? Have *they* responded with love and understanding, rather than with judgment and rejection? Have *they* found enough support that they can begin speaking the truth to others and to their child, set firm boundaries for their child's behavior to maintain the safety of their home, and taken the courageous stands necessary to protect his or her health and safety?

The detached parent is deeply caring, deeply empathetic, holds the child fully responsible for making the choices necessary to get sober, and no longer enables addictive behavior by artificially softening the natural consequences of poor choices. Detached parents make the tough choices themselves, without regard for how their child (and others) will perceive them. They detach from the outcome of their behavior, meaning that they recognize they have no power to force certain results. They do what they *know* is right and let the results take care of themselves. Through giving and receiving support in Al-Anon, parents gain the experience and knowledge needed to be comfortable with the hard decisions demanded of them.

This is the preparation needed if we are going to have a strong chance of intervening successfully in a child's addiction. Being prepared does not guarantee that we will be effective. Nothing can guarantee that a child will ever see the reasons for sobriety or the path to get there. Being prepared means only that we have given ourselves the best chance to be effective and have thereby given our children the best help humanly available.

Are there statistics proving Al-Anon's effectiveness? No. The most relevant data comes from many studies proving that chemical dependence treatment programs that include a family component are more effective. Most treatment programs base their family approach on the principles pioneered by Al-Anon and encourage participation in Al-Anon meetings. I have focused primarily on Al-Anon's approach, although other approaches exist, such as those that emphasize tough love. Most of these alternative approaches have much in common with Al-Anon, but none is as generally available in every community. It is safe to assume that, whether Al-Anon fits you perfectly or not, you are likely to have to struggle with many of its perspectives as you prepare to intervene in your child's behavior.

The Goals of Intervention

Vernon Johnson, a leader in developing treatment for alcoholism, first developed the formal process of intervening in a family member's addiction. His 1986 book *Intervention* was subtitled *How to Help Someone Who Doesn't Want Help.* Formal intervention is designed to confront alcoholic adults in a supportive way, and the goal is to get the addict to accept the need for treatment. Another author and counselor, Dick Schaefer, tailored intervention to better meet the needs of adolescents and described the process in his 1987 book *Choices and Consequences.* Schaefer created a process that includes a series of contracts (detailed later in this section) and that teaches teens to take greater responsibility for themselves, to look ahead to see the consequences of their choices, and then to prove either that they are able to abide by the rules they have agreed to or that they need protection and help in a treatment program.

What are the legitimate goals of intervening in a teen's marijuana dependence? "Legitimate" means "realistic." It is not realistic to intervene on a child's addiction with the expectation that the family is going to return to its *status quo ante*—that is, to precisely the way life was before addiction entered the scene. Life can get better than it ever was for both the adolescent and the whole family. But too much has happened to return to earlier, more naive times. That would not be a realistic goal for intervention and would produce only disappointment.

There are three clear and achievable goals for intervention. In the order in which they can be achieved, the goals of intervention are

- dismantling denial
- achieving abstinence
- entering recovery

Denial

Denial needs to be "dismantled" because it is a wall that has been constructed to keep the truth at bay. Most every teen who has slipped into marijuana dependence will be steeped in denial. Parents have their own denial as well. When denial is present, we can't believe the evidence that is clearly before us. We can't believe the evidence because we don't want to believe it. The evidence points toward a conclusion—whether about one's own drug use or about an adolescent's behavior—that we are not ready to deal with. We may not be willing to feel the emotions, especially the fear and sadness, that will be triggered by acknowledging the truth. Or we may be staving off harsh anger and judgment we don't ever want to hold toward someone we love so deeply. We may avoid seeing the truth because we can't bear the shame we will feel.

Whatever the unconscious reasons parents have for building up a protective shield of denial, intervention must begin in themselves. It begins by looking squarely at each piece of evidence that addiction may be present. If parents have detached sufficiently, they can begin seeing the real implications of a child's behavior. When enough signs are present—erratic behavior, loss of usual interests, declining school performance, loss of old friends, changing values, increased hostility, mood swings, and severe emotional distress—dismantling denial means coming to the conclusion that addiction has taken over. Al-Anon helps in this process of breaking denial. Consultation with a professional experienced in treating adolescent addiction may also prove invaluable.

Abstinence

Addiction is a state of mind, resulting from a change in brain chemistry that is qualitatively different from normal. When a person is using harmful amounts of alcohol or other drugs but has not reached the point of addiction yet, he or she can often successfully reduce his or her use back to safe levels. This proves impossible once people develop full-blown chemical dependence. The best evidence, supplied by George Vallaint in *The Natural History of Alcoholism—Revisited*, shows that those alcoholics who appear to control their drinking for as much as five years eventually choose total abstinence or almost invariably reactivate their full addiction. As noted in chapter 3, marijuana dependence literally causes structural changes in the reward center, making even occasional use potentially problematic. Total abstinence is the prescription given by most addiction specialists to arrest addictive disease, in the same way that allergists prescribe total abstinence from shrimp for people who have developed a life-threatening allergy to shellfish.

Confronting teens with all the evidence that eventually broke through our own denial is the next step, but it is unrealistic to anticipate that this will automatically inspire them to seek treatment. Occasionally teens have become so desperate that they jump at the chance to get help. So we need to be ready to respond. We need to be familiar with local therapists and treatment programs available for adolescents. The willingness to acknowledge their addiction is a great start but does not mean that the adolescents fully understand all the implications of being addicted or what steps will be necessary to stop using. They will need lots of help, and knowing that their parents support them enough to be familiar with the available resources will feel good. The work has just begun, for the teens and their family as a whole.

More often, adolescents will remain in denial, facing us with the challenge of having to set clear limits to promote abstinence. The task is to take back control of our environment in ways that begin backing a teen into a corner of his or her own making. Schaefer calls this the *simple contract* stage. We establish the rules in a written agreement: *no drug or alcohol use, no violence (physical or verbal), and no cutting school.* In addition, we need to find a way for the teen to be exposed to *basic information about marijuana* in particular and addiction in general. This may come from a basic information class at a nearby treatment program, a group run by a local therapist specializing in adolescent addiction, or simply a therapist who will meet individually for an agreed-upon number of sessions to provide basic education. Whatever environment is found for this education, it needs to have the capacity to conduct random *urine screens* to monitor whether abstinence is truly achieved.

The simple contract is not complete unless it clearly outlines specific and concrete consequences for breaking any of the rules. In most cases, failure to abide by the contract needs to have the consequence of undergoing a formal chemical dependence evaluation at either an outpatient or inpatient treatment program. The goal is abstinence—from drug use and other basic unacceptable behaviors. If the teen chooses against abstinence, he or she knows precisely what the consequences will be. In exchange for keeping agreements outlined in the contract, more major changes remain unnecessary. And the teen's life can proceed with a minimum of additional restrictions or monitoring.

The simple contract may be sufficient if a teen is still in the stage of seeking the mood swing. But it is likely to be broken if he or she has become addicted, since pot use has become more central to his or her life at that point than reearning his or her parents' trust. Once the first contract has been broken, it is necessary to set stricter limits. Schaefer calls the next contract a *turf contract*. It contains all the elements of the simple contract and further outlines specific behaviors required to earn privileges (e.g., a later curfew, use of television, telephone, car). The behaviors can include tasks around the house, personal cleanliness, dress, and the like. It is important that the behaviors be clearly delineated and easily monitored by parents. Trying to control the people a teenager is socializing with at school is impossible to monitor, while requiring a clean room before leaving home is easy to monitor. There is room for negotiation of which behaviors (but not which privileges) are to be included in the new contract. Again, the consequences need to be clearly understood. If the teen chooses to break the turf contract, he or she will enter formal treatment, in either an inpatient or outpatient setting.

Schaefer also outlines a *bottom-line contract* to be used if a teen does not adhere to the turf contract above. When, despite being given information about addiction and being closely monitored, a teen continues to use pot, it is time to question whether he or she can retain the privilege of living at home and remaining in the current school environment. The bottom-line contract offers a teen one more chance. It clearly outlines the behaviors that must be met if he or she wishes to avoid the consequence of being admitted to an inpatient treatment center, being enrolled in a therapeutic wilderness program, or attending a therapeutic boarding school. The actual consequences depend to a large extent on a family's or a school system's resources. A lot of thought and planning need to go into arranging the consequences for violating a bottom-line contract. The goal for all three contracts is the same, however—helping an adolescent abandon denial and choose abstinence, as well as helping parents to become informed about the depth of their child's dependence on pot.

Some parents may be convinced that the contracting approach outlined in this section, with its emphasis on behavior and consequences, would not work with their children. Specifically, they may argue that their children act out when they feel bad about themselves and what is needed is reassurance that they are wonderful, beautiful people who are loved no matter what they do. If their children were not dependent on marijuana, they might be right. But addiction is a state of mind that is qualitatively different from normal. Once addiction takes hold of teens, it creates unexpectedly deep ruptures in their relationships. The proper boundaries between parent and child are usually obscured and need to be rebuilt. The process of contracting, with defined consequences for behaviors that can be clearly monitored, may initially appear heavy-handed and infantilizing. But it is the most direct route to reestablishing necessary boundaries and providing teens the means to demonstrate their willingness to become trustworthy.

Recovery

Breaking denial and becoming abstinent are just the beginning. As great an achievement as they represent, they amount only to getting into the starting blocks. Recovery—the building of a full, rich, and gratifying life without marijuana—still lies ahead for the child. Without recovery, life remains static, like being left at the starting line after the gun has sounded while the others have dashed ahead.

Recovery and healing are also necessary for most parents. Months, and sometimes years, have usually been spent feeling overly responsible for a child's marijuana use and ashamed of his or her behavior. Efforts to control their child have taken a toll on parents' self-esteem. Resentments linger from disappointed expectations and do not easily fade with time, or even with a child's abstinence. The work of recovery is needed to find lasting forgiveness for the pain a child has caused as well as for the mistakes and failings a parent has contributed.

Chapter 10 explores recovery in detail. For the moment, two points are important. First, recovery is a realistic goal of intervention. Unless we aim high, we jeopardize abstinence. The goal of recovery is to safeguard abstinence, to solidify it, and to build a successful life on the foundation of abstinence. This is not too much to ask or too much to hope for. Some parents see the deep personal work needed to make progress in recovery and conclude that recovery demands more of adolescents than they are capable of. This dim view sells teens short. *Never underestimate a teenager's ability to maintain abstinence or to achieve deep recovery.*

The second point is that recovery from addiction is different for adolescents than for adults. In adult treatment programs we speak of *rehabilitation.* This concept implies that we are aiming to help recovering adults regain the skills and strengths they previously had, before addiction destroyed their integrity. But adolescent addicts cannot be *rehabilitated* because they are still in the process of being *habilitated* to begin with. Adolescents in recovery have no solid "before addiction" identity to return to. Recovery is imperative for abstinent adolescents to begin making up the developmental ground they lost when using. This means demanding, sometimes painful, and almost always very personal work. But the period immediately following abstinence is often a time of great flexibility and openness to change and an opportunity to make giant developmental leaps. This is not a time to underestimate teens' abilities but rather to support them in the greatest undertaking of their lives.

A Framework for Talking to Your Teen

It is one thing to understand the goals of intervention and how creating contracts that focus on behavior and consequences can help reach these goals. But sometimes the simple act of *talking* with a child has become so awkward that parents don't know where to start. The atmosphere between parents and child can range anywhere from frigid to overheated or may bounce erratically between the two extremes. Some families may still maintain at least a pretense of honest relationships; a veneer of civility still reigns despite the adolescent's secret life. At the other end of the spectrum, some families will be in a state of open warfare. In either case, parents can feel tremendous anxiety at the prospect of speaking openly to their child. *"What will the response be? What if we're wrong, despite all the evidence we have? What if we cause an even bigger explosion?"* The stakes seem high—because they are high.

Whatever has become of the family atmosphere, there are certain basic principles that are helpful for talking to teens in trouble with drugs. We need to focus on the *love* that keeps us struggling to safeguard our child's health and safety, on the *respect* we have for his or her freedom to make choices, and the *reality* of what his or her behavior has been. These three words—love, respect, and reality—help keep us focused on the goal when a child's sarcastic response or caustic disregard for what we are saying threatens to knock us off course. Confronting out of anger will be more destructive than constructive because it will drive the child away. It will feel more hurtful than caring. And it runs the risk of expressing the punitive part of our nature, despite our best intentions. If we are not able to confront our child out of love, it is best that we work on ourselves first. But we cannot delay confronting the truth for too long without increasing the risk to our child.

The following framework for conversations with our child may guide us to the best outcome possible.

I Care

We begin by telling a teen how much we care about him or her. This expression of love has to be more than a preface. It has to be more than, "I love you, *but* . . ." We need to reach deep within ourselves and remember the profound bond we have with our child, no matter how hostile the relationship might currently be. This is not primarily an expression of concern for his or her health, which will likely be seen as a veiled criticism. It is a time to make simple declarations. "I love you, *and* it matters deeply to me whether you are happy. More than anything, I hope you can feel how much I care for you."

I See

Then we tell them what we see and what we hear that leads us to be concerned. We have to prepare carefully for this portion of any intervention. Our tendency is to pour out a maelstrom of our fears. We often start with our conclusions ("You are addicted") rather than the facts. It is useful to work with a professional to practice presenting what we see. The goal is to be specific. For example, "Last Friday you said you were going to be at your friend's house and that you would be home by eleven o'clock. You did not get home until after two o'clock and you avoided us as much as you could. We smelled smoke on your breath and what you were saying didn't make much sense to us." Or, "After you left for school this morning, I smelled marijuana smoke coming from your room. When I looked inside, I found this pipe." The more concrete and specific your observations can be, the more blatant a child's denial (or lying) has to become if he or she is still going to hide from the truth.

I Feel

Now is the time to confront the teen with how we feel about what we have seen. We cannot blame our feelings on the child. They are our emotional reactions to the facts. This can be a difficult step. We may be tempted to say, "You *made* me feel scared." This is not true. Other parents may have seen the same facts and not felt scared at all. The fear, or the sadness, is *ours*. *We* do the feeling. This is the step when we simply communicate, in a nonjudgmental, nonblaming manner, what we felt when we saw the behavior. For example, "When I found the pipe in your room, I felt shocked and betrayed, and then I started feeling really mad." Or, "When you were not home at the time you said you would be, I began feeling scared. My fear kept growing until I finally heard you come in the door."

I Want

We need to be clear about what we want a child to do and what behaviors we want him or her to change. This takes preparation, and again, professional guidance can be helpful. Before the intervention, we need to be clear what contract we want our child to make with us. Once we are convinced our child has become chemically dependent, we certainly want all marijuana, alcohol, and other drug use to stop. We don't have to have absolute scientific certainty that abstinence is the only safe course to know that we want our child to take this more prudent course for the time being. If our child denies smoking pot, we can give him or her the opportunity to prove that he or she is clean and sober. This usually means arranging with a professional to monitor use by urine screens. *"Don't you trust me?!"* our teen may shout indignantly. The best answer tends to be that trust is not the real issue;

his or her use is the issue. If our child is trustworthy, this will be easily proven by clean test results and our trust will be earned. We may want our child to cooperate with evaluation of his or her marijuana use by a chemical dependence professional. We may want our child to enter treatment, either on an outpatient basis or in a residential program, if this is a professional's recommendation. Any ambiguity or ambivalence on our part will destroy the message. Any differences in the message delivered by two parents will be exploited to the detriment of the message. Preparation is key. We need to know what we want before we get into conversation with our child, because teens will try to negotiate us out of whatever limits they possibly can.

I Will

We end with a clear statement about what we will do to support our child's efforts to abstain from pot and get his or her life back on track. We may agree to hire a tutor for help catching up with schoolwork. We may agree to help find a counselor our child feels comfortable confiding in or a treatment program with other teens who are struggling with sobriety. And sometimes it means promising to get ourselves to Al-Anon, to learn how to back off from trying to control every part of our child's life, to deal with our resentments, and to begin looking at how our behavior could be improved. Interventions end by looping back to the beginning, to expressions of our caring for the person we feel is in trouble. The final message is "I will support you because I care about what happens to you."

Mobilizing Outside Help

A saying among the recovering community is "We are only as sick as our secrets." This recognizes how common the impulse is to hide problems but how dangerous this tendency is to health. Addicts are not the only ones who try to keep their behavior secret. Whole families frequently go to great lengths to keep their dirty laundry from being aired in public. As a result, however, parents sometimes engage in a losing battle with their drug-abusing teenagers without getting the outside support and expertise they so desperately need.

In considering whether an intervention is necessary to help a teenager addicted to pot, we are often fighting against an entire culture. The local drug culture, composed of peers, dealers, and local businesses that sell paraphernalia, books, CDs, and concerts, works against us. The media works against us. Newscasts work against us by running stories about medical marijuana with enticing visuals of fresh bud and people lighting up and getting high. Isolated families are frequently no match for all the counterforces. It takes active support from a community to counterbalance the drug culture.

When we as parents face the challenge of helping our children return from the loss of perspective induced by their pot smoking, it is time to forget about keeping secrets. It is time to begin mobilizing whatever support might be available throughout the wider community. We can turn in the following directions for help.

Getting Family Counseling

It is often helpful to make appointments with a counselor who is skilled in working with families, even if the whole family is not willing to attend sessions. The message this delivers is that both parents are going to actively pursue change for the family, whether everyone is on board or not. So if someone wants to be part of determining what direction things are going, he or she might want to participate.

Talking to the Extended Family

It is time to stop hiding our pain from our brothers and sisters or from our parents. We need support, too. It is foolish to isolate ourselves from the rest of our family's support in order to "protect" a child's reputation. Recovery begins for everyone who is willing to start being honest and dealing with what is real. An adolescent may feel betrayed by being "tattled" on to his or her grandparents, aunts, and uncles. But if he or she were doing nothing to be embarrassed about, there would be nothing troubling to tell.

Talking to Other Parents

Most of us would expect the parents of our child's best friend to let us know if their child was getting into trouble with marijuana. We probably would not like learning after the fact that our son or daughter was being exposed to a risk that could have been avoided. We would not like being excluded from helping a kid who needed help. And we would not like the damage done to the sense of community that occurs when parents hide from each other. We might even feel betrayed. We have an obligation to communicate with other parents about adolescent drug use every bit as much as we would about a case of chicken pox or mumps. Furthermore, we need the support of as many other parents as possible to help set effective limits for a child who needs help.

Talking to Teachers and Coaches

Adolescent marijuana use flourishes in an atmosphere of denial, ignorance, and secrets. It would not make sense to hide a child's dyslexia from teachers or to keep his or her asthma a secret from a coach. Again, kids who are smoking pot most likely won't like having the rest of the community know. We may not be able to control what our children do, but we can often have a lot of influence over the environment in which they do it.

Talking to a Spiritual Leader

If we receive comfort and guidance from a religious tradition, we may benefit from speaking openly and often to the leader of our congregation, parish, synagogue, mosque, or temple. In the past some religious leaders took a moralistic approach to addiction and only added to a family's shame. What we need instead is our spiritual leader's caring, guidance, and help in sustaining the faith that we are truly pursuing our child's best interests. At a minimum, speaking to a spiritual leader further erases the isolation and darkness that tends to envelop families in crisis. In most cases, leaders should be able to connect us with others in the religious community who have weathered the same storms. Fortunately, today most clergy are better trained in addiction. The stories we bring won't be new to clergy; they've heard the story many times before and have heard far worse cases than most parents can imagine. The message the spirit needs to hear is clear: None of us is alone.

When the Police Have a Role

Parents may fail to see the police as helpers. Parents may do anything to avoid having their children come to the authorities' attention. The message this gives, both to children and to themselves, is that families are isolated from their community. This isolation disconnects their parental authority from any communal authority, when it is our communities that can help set and maintain clear standards. Many communities have curfews, and parents have the legal right to enforce these curfews. In fact, as much as adolescents despise the fact, parents have broad legal authority to determine where and how their children will live.

When one family discovered that their fourteen-year-old daughter had sneaked out after 11:00 P.M., they called her cell phone, which she answered. They told her to get home within fifteen minutes or they would call the police to report her absence. She arrived home seventeen minutes later, as the parents were on the phone to the police. When the police asked whether to come out anyway, the parents said yes. They were aware that unenforced limits soon become hollow threats to teens. The police arrived and explained that the parents could lodge a complaint and the police would cite their daughter for a curfew violation if the parents wished. The consequences of being cited were clearly explained and involved having to meet with an investigator from juvenile justice services. When the parents decided not to lodge a complaint this time, but stated they would ask for their daughter to be cited if she sneaked out again, the daughter had every reason to believe her parents would follow through. The police are sometimes necessary to provide the community's formal support for parental authority. Refusal to involve the police is a decision to relinquish some of our legitimate authority to set limits for our children.

Finding Professional Help

Being an informed consumer of mental health and addiction services is difficult. First, clear standards don't exist for evaluating the competency of therapists and counselors. There is no *Consumer Reports* magazine to rate national "brands" of therapy the way we might when choosing a car. Second, if we are looking for help, we're probably in distress and don't have much time to educate ourselves fully before committing to working with a professional. We probably feel vulnerable because of the immediacy of our needs. To delay choosing a counselor is to run the risk of permitting problems to deepen by our inaction.

In most cases, the best recommendations will come from parents who have recently faced the same problem, and we can find these parents at Al-Anon meetings. Raising our hand at a meeting and sharing what is happening to our family gives us an opportunity to ask anyone who has found good professional help to speak to us after the meeting. We will almost certainly carry a handful of suggested names of professionals (and of Al-Anon members willing to give us the benefit of their experience) home with us.

There are several other sources of referrals for professional help in any community. Call local school counselors and ask them for names of professionals who are known to work well with teens. Call the closest alcohol and drug treatment programs, outpatient and residential, and ask about their services and any counselors or therapists who have entered private practice in the area after having worked at their center. If the nearest residential treatment center is too distant to use, we can ask where they refer patients from our area for aftercare (i.e., ongoing treatment after finishing an inpatient treatment program). Halfway houses that specialize in providing sober living environments for people in recovery from addiction are also good sources of information about the local professional community.

Most of these resources can be found in the telephone directory's Yellow Pages, along with an Al-Anon number under "Alcoholism." (However, do not expect to receive any referrals to professionals through Al-Anon's offices. The Twelve Step programs have a tradition prohibiting them from getting involved in any outside controversies, such as which treatment centers and counselors might be the best.) Finally, the American Society of Addiction Medicine (www.asam.org) and the American Academy of Addiction Psychiatry (www.aaap.org) have Web sites that list physicians throughout the United States who have a special interest and expertise in addiction. Many of them can steer parents toward useful resources in their local communities.

Some of us may have started seeing a therapist before it became clear that marijuana use is an important ingredient in our family's problems. How will we know whether the professional we have already begun to build a relationship with is skilled in working with chemical dependence? Since we are probably early in our education about marijuana and adolescent addiction, we may not be able to assess how prepared the therapist is to lead us through some difficult terrain. A few questions may help us decide. Has the therapist had any specialized training in chemical dependence beyond the introduction most training programs provide today? Has the therapist been supervised in any chemical dependence cases or worked in any treatment programs? What percentage of his or her practice focuses on addiction? How comfortable is the therapist working with adolescents who are abusing drugs? What community resources and treatment programs does he or she rely on to help addicted adolescents who need more intense treatment? How does the therapist feel about Twelve Step programs such as Alcoholics Anonymous, Marijuana Anonymous (MA), or Al-Anon? And, perhaps most important, we can observe how comfortable the therapist is with our questions. Do we sense any defensiveness, or is the therapist open about his or her limits and confident about his or her skills?

The ultimate judge of whether a specific professional is competent lies with each of us. We need to feel that our concerns as parents are being taken seriously, but also that the professional has the confidence to call us to task when our own thinking is distorted. We need to develop a sense that the professional has "seen it all before" and will not be manipulated by a verbal, powerful adolescent who is still in denial. But we also need to believe that the professional has enough ability to relate to teens to eventually gain our child's trust. And, very important, we need a professional who is able to give direction to what has often become a chaotic situation—to teach us about addiction, to lead us through the specific steps of contracting and intervention, and perhaps also to lead us through the maze of available outpatient and inpatient treatment programs.

Finally, it is often best to rely on the professional to take control over whether urine testing is appropriate for monitoring a teen. An increasing array of drug testing products is becoming available for home use. At the same time, an increasing array of products for defeating drug testing is available to teens interested in avoiding detection. The whole issue of urine testing is fertile ground for immense family power struggles, especially when observed specimens are necessary. Deceit and recrimination are often the result more than useful information about whether a teen is smoking pot. In many, if not most, cases this power struggle is best sidestepped by having a counselor take responsibility for determining when and how to conduct urine screens. A skilled professional is in a far better position than parents to turn the testing process into a therapeutic opportunity.

Summary and Checklist

The younger a child is when beginning to smoke marijuana, the more likely it is that he or she will become one of the minority of smokers who experience serious threats to their health and safety. Parents need to seek support from their community to become clear about what limits can realistically be set for their children. Al-Anon is an important resource for helping parents detach and focus on keeping their own behavior sane while attempting to intervene in a child's addiction. The goals of intervention are the breaking of denial, establishment of abstinence, and entering into recovery (which, for adolescents, means catching up with neglected developmental tasks).

Schaefer's book *Choices and Consequences* outlines a series of contracts to make with adolescents to set a progression of whatever limits and consequences are necessary to protect their health and safety. The framework to use in confronting teenagers is to focus on love and respect for them while expressing concern about the behavior parents see putting them at risk, how parents feel about their behavior, what parents want from them, and what parents are willing to do to support these changes. Many resources are available to support parents dealing with addicted adolescents. They can seek family counseling; talk honestly to their extended family, other parents, teachers, coaches, and spiritual leaders; and involve the police when necessary. While it is often difficult for parents to find professional counselors they are comfortable with and confident in, there are several sources for useful referrals. The best referrals tend to come from parents attending Al-Anon who have had direct experience with professional help in confronting addiction in their own children.

The following checklist may help parents organize their efforts:

_____ Attend at least six Al-Anon meetings
_____ Read Dick Schaefer's *Choices and Consequences*
_____ Develop a list of local treatment programs, outpatient and inpatient
_____ Develop a list of counselors and therapists experienced in adolescent addiction
_____ Arrange for a professional to conduct urine screens, if needed
_____ Have at least one "I care, I see, I feel, I want, I will" conversation with my child
_____ Begin contracting with my child
_____ Return to Al-Anon to work more on detaching
_____ Start family counseling
_____ Talk to extended family
_____ Talk to other parents
_____ Talk to teachers and coaches
_____ Talk to spiritual leader
_____ Contact police to discuss what role they are willing to play

Chapter 9

Treatment: What to Expect

Conventional wisdom among pot smokers in the 1960s was that cannabis was harmless and not addictive. At that point, alcoholism treatment was still in its infancy, and treatment centers still largely ignored tobacco use. At the same time, Twelve Step recovery communities such as Alcoholics Anonymous (thirty years old in 1965) recognized that the psychoactive properties of pot are antithetical to sobriety. Most recovering people did not have any doubt, even during the sixties, that using marijuana would threaten their recovery.

By 1999 the landscape involving treatment of marijuana dependence had changed substantially. That year, according to a Drug and Alcohol Services Information System report, more than 220,000 people were admitted to publicly funded programs for treatment of marijuana addiction, fully 14 percent of all admissions for alcohol and other drug treatment at these facilities.[1] In 1993 the admission rate in the United States for primary marijuana treatment was 55 per 100,000 for persons in the general population twelve or older. In 1996 the rate was 91 per 100,000. By 1999 the rate had risen to 103 per 100,000. What has been shifting?

Following are several contributors to the increase in treatment for marijuana dependence.

- The age of initial use has been declining, leading to more high-risk young teens being exposed to marijuana.

- The treatment field has gradually shifted from a primary focus on alcohol to a wider scope encompassing all drugs of abuse. We now speak of *chemical dependence* in general, recognizing that all chemical addictions appear to have a common core. This shift was also necessitated by the fact that there are very few "pure alcoholics" anymore. Most addicts use multiple drugs, including alcohol.

- The criminal justice system is increasingly likely to mandate treatment rather than jail or prison when someone is arrested for a nonviolent drug-related crime.

- The marijuana available today has up to ten times more THC than the pot from the sixties. Antimarijuana forces sometimes argue that today's pot is so strong, it has become an entirely different drug. This is no more true than claiming that the alcohol molecule in vodka is different from the alcohol molecule in beer. On the other hand, the effect of gulping a glass of vodka *is* far greater than gulping the same amount of beer. A high concentration of THC means faster delivery, and faster delivery leads to more intense effects.

Reasons to Enter Treatment

An essential element of treatment for marijuana or any other drug dependence is creation of the *patient role*. When people accept the patient role, they are acknowledging the existence of a problem and their need for help. When we grant people the patient role, we remove the burden of shame by acknowledging that they have been overwhelmed by some force outside their control (whether an infection, a cancer, or an addicting chemical). We approach patients with compassion, not with judgment or moralism. And we provide patients with the means for healing, whether that be an antibiotic, an operation, or education. In the case of treatment for chemical dependence, we offer patients asylum and protection from the stresses of their world when this is needed (including protection from being exposed to the presence of alcohol and other drugs). We offer support, psychological evaluation, education, techniques for managing stress, group and individual counseling, medication when appropriate, family therapy, and access to Twelve Step programs. Then treatment holds patients accountable for how they make use of these tools. The modern patient role is not passive. Whether a postsurgical patient is expected to work hard in physical rehabilitation or a diabetic is expected to lose weight and take responsibility for diet and exercise or an addict is expected to work a serious program of recovery, the patient role demands active participation in one's healing.

Marijuana users enter treatment with several complaints in common. These include

- loss of control of use
- cognitive and motivational impairment
- decline in occupational and academic performance
- decreased self-esteem
- depression
- complaint of a partner or parent

This list does not differ significantly from the complaints that bring people into treatment for alcoholism or addiction to other drugs. The main difference is the absence of severe symptoms such as withdrawal (alcohol, cocaine, and opiates), seizures (alcohol), overdoses (opiates), and hallucinations and paranoia (cocaine and speed). The reality is that, although pot can adversely affect maturation, concentration, memory, mood, relationships, and spiritual health, it is physically far less harsh than most other drugs. Pot is less immediately devastating to the brain and to the rest of the body than "harder" drugs, including alcohol.

Another noteworthy aspect of the preceding complaints is the inclusion of "cognitive and motivational impairment." Alcoholics often experience cognitive impairment, especially as addiction advances into their later years, but these impairments usually come to light only during treatment. Few alcoholics enter treatment already complaining of cognitive difficulties. Also, opiates such as Vicodin and heroin diminish motivation, but few opiate addicts list lack of motivation as an important reason for entering treatment, primarily because more apparent reasons (such as overdosing, chronic withdrawal, arrest, or infection) stand out as reasons for seeking treatment.

Marijuana smokers, on the other hand, *do* often become aware of their diminished involvement in the world. While many users "drop out," many others maintain enough perspective to observe themselves falling out of step with their peers. This is perhaps easiest for adolescents to sense because the rate of change during this period of life is inherently so rapid. The lack of motivation, which is more accurately seen as a relative inability to experience novelty unless stoned, contributes heavily to the development of depression and low self-esteem.

Changes That Occur in Treatment

Adolescents I have seen coming out of treatment for marijuana dependence tend to describe the benefits of abstinence in similar ways. Perhaps surprisingly, this seems to be true whether their treatment was entered voluntarily or was coerced. Although the fact that forced treatment can have the same impact as voluntary treatment seems to violate common sense, these results are consistent with numerous studies on alcohol treatment, where it has been demonstrated that the success rate is equal for those who enter voluntarily and for those whose treatment is court mandated. The benefits of treatment for pot include

- clarity, clarity, clarity: lifting of the fog
- recognition of past denial
- freedom
- improved relationships

The best way to illustrate the changes that treatment can produce is to look in detail at two individuals, Henry and Karen. The following vignettes trace their descent into dependence on marijuana, treatment, and their reemergence into a sober life.

Henry

Henry was twelve years old when he first smoked marijuana. He did not have to be talked into trying pot by his best friend, whose older brother kept a stash in his bedroom. No, Henry was eager to see what the fuss was about. He had heard many older kids talk about getting high and it sounded exciting, like being one of the first to try snowboarding or to shoplift a candy bar. Henry had been a risk taker his whole life, fearless and attracted to excitement. He was also severely affected by attention deficit disorder (ADD) but had steadfastly refused to accept that he had the condition or to take any medication. He had rationalized his impulsivity as arising from a special connection with his unconscious that permitted him to be more spontaneously natural than others who had already become constrained by the oppressive dictates of social norms. When others took offense at being interrupted, Henry chalked the reactions up to their difficulty with being faced by the truths contained in the unfiltered associations his mind blurted out. He did not see himself as having any problems personally. I found it nearly impossible to connect with Henry and could see how tightly he was locked out of relationships by a combination of his ADD and all the rationalizations he had built around it. His constant marijuana use by that point had not caused his isolation but had gravely complicated my attempt to reach him.

Henry was immediately attracted to the mood swing he experienced with pot, as well as to its stimulation of novelty. Since his ADD made attending to mundane tasks difficult for him, the artificially enhanced sense of novelty provided by pot was pleasant and gave him the impression that marijuana was the perfect medication for his ADD (which he paradoxically still denied having). He did not seem to notice any effect on memory by the pot, but this could be explained by the fact that his severe ADD already made it difficult for him to maintain continuity in his experience. Within weeks, Henry was smoking marijuana every day and beginning to experiment with ways to smoke it throughout the day. At other times, when forced to be with the family all day, he demonstrated to himself that he did not *have* to smoke it.

From the family's perspective, not a lot changed with Henry at first. He seemed more inward and calm than usual, which was welcome. Within a few months, however, the quality and quantity of his schoolwork took a plunge. Teachers began contacting his parents to report failing performance and frequent absences (which was entirely new for Henry). His behavior was becoming more problematic in other ways, both at school and home. Previously he had often been disruptive because of his continual restlessness, impulsivity, and inability to listen attentively. Now he was becoming disdainful, defiant, and openly hostile. Emotions tended to erupt from him, escalating even minor episodes into crises. His entire sleep/wake cycle was reversing, as he tended to sleep most of the day and stay up all night, often sneaking out of the house. He disregarded any restrictions or punishments his parents tried to place on him. In addition, Henry began to be more careless about hiding his marijuana smoking. His parents found roaches (the leftover butts of smoked joints) and burned matches in his room. Campus security caught him smoking on school grounds. When the police investigated, they found several ounces of marijuana in Henry's locker, enough that they arrested him for dealing. From the time he first tried marijuana to the time he was put on probation took a year and a half.

The third time Henry's urine screen came up positive for THC while on probation, the drug court judge gave him a choice: juvenile hall for six months or admission to an adolescent residential drug treatment program in a rural part of the state. Henry reluctantly chose treatment. More accurately, Henry rejected juvenile hall. He decided that he could tolerate a drug program more easily than being locked up in "juvie."

The last time I saw Henry before he left for treatment he was dressed in baggy pants and a T-shirt that sported a huge marijuana leaf. He slumped on the couch, hands in pockets. His gaze rarely met mine and his eyelids hung at half-mast, either from being stoned at the moment or from his utter exhaustion, I wasn't sure which. He was insolent and challenging, sarcastic and dismissing. He argued with whatever I said and labeled my comments "dumb" whenever he didn't have an immediate retort. He steadfastly defended his marijuana use. He frequently repeated himself as though this strengthened his point.

I next met with Henry three months later, soon after he was discharged from treatment. He wore the same baggy pants, but a plain hooded sweatshirt had replaced the T-shirt. He sat up and made direct eye contact throughout our conversation. When I asked him to describe the effect, good, bad, or indifferent, of being marijuana-free for more than ninety days, Henry replied, "My mind is clear." He went on to describe a fog that had permeated his head while smoking but that he had been unable to see until after he had gotten clean. His description reminded me of a quote in Andrew Weil's book *The Natural Mind:* Marijuana is "insidious as a creator of illusion, for it enables the user to pretend that he is not really dependent on it at the same time that it reinforces the notion that highs come in joints."[2] Henry had fallen into that illusion and had been convinced that smoking more pot was the only way to pierce through the fog. By being continuously stoned, he had lost awareness of how clouded his mind had become. The "positive" impact pot had on his ADD made it harder for Henry to see the cognitive impairments that many other pot smokers notice.

He still did not like school. He still thought that the police were repressive and that it was unjust to outlaw marijuana while permitting alcohol to be legal. But he was committed, for the time being, to abstaining from all mood-altering drugs. Why? Henry said that he enjoyed the feeling of freedom that being clean gave him. Some of the freedom came from knowing that his parents, or even the police, could search his pockets or go through his room or his locker and he had nothing to fear, nothing to hide. But there was also a deeper sense of freedom that came from a combination of being clean and having been placed on the proper medications for his ADD while in treatment. He saw now, for the first time, how much his ADD had limited him. He enjoyed the freedom that comes from being able to refrain from acting on every impulse and said, "I have a better chance to be myself when I'm not reacting all the time."

During family week at the treatment center, Henry had finally come out of denial about how much pot smoking, and ADD, had colored his relationship with his parents. Without the fog permeating his brain, Henry was able to experience the concern that his folks felt for him. He was also able to let some of the warmth that he still felt for them come to the surface. It was easier to get back in touch with his own desire to be a kid again, with parents who loved him, while in the supportive treatment environment. Being surrounded by other kids who were also emerging from their own drug use and reconnecting with their natural longing for affection enabled Henry to do the same. He liked the current lack of warfare between himself and his parents.

Karen

Karen, fourteen years old, first smoked marijuana and tried alcohol during the summer between eighth and ninth grade. A delightful, intelligent, outgoing girl who never lacked for friends, Karen had the misfortune of fully entering puberty early in fifth grade. While the other girls in her class had not yet developed, Karen was receiving stares and taunts from all the curious boys. By the time she was thirteen, she looked seventeen. Peers misinterpreted the boys' undisguised sexual interest in her as part of Karen's identity. She was the target throughout middle school of sexual harassment by boys who didn't yet possess the conceptual ability to comprehend how their behavior was affecting her. Nor did they care.

In high school, Karen was presented the opportunity to ride to new levels of popularity on the magic carpet of her body. Junior and senior boys showed her and a few other attractive freshmen girls a lot of attention. She was dizzy with excitement at being able to leave behind the immaturity of boys her own age in exchange for entry into a world of parties, riding around in cars, and the attention of older, more sophisticated boys. Of course, parties meant being introduced to pot and alcohol. The older boys also expected her to be sexually active, which was easier for her and more likely to happen when stoned. Within six months, the social whirl had swept her away from her previous interests in school and sports. The pain of being seduced and then dropped, passed around and then passed over, was quickly salved by smoking whenever she could. Her family's strong history of addiction had found its way into her genes, which responded quickly. She soon lost control of how much and when she was using. Her emotions alternated between great intensity and apathy.

As Karen's parents became concerned and began pulling in the reins on her social activities, Karen rebelled with outbursts of hostility that scared even herself. Within a single hour she could be screaming vile insults at her mother, then crying in despair, apologizing earnestly, and again screaming when her mother's expression of concern was seen as more criticism. The stress of her own emotional intensity began wearing Karen down. She could go days without caring for her hygiene, moping hopelessly in her room, and then a new boy would look her way and the world would brighten with an explosion of light and hope. In either state, depressed or enthralled, she neglected her schoolwork.

Toward the end of her ninth-grade year, Karen was failing two and possibly three classes, was sneaking out of the house at night, and could not control her pot use. Karen had been seeing a therapist throughout the year, but it became apparent that she had been lying to her most of the time. To intervene in a situation that had flown out of control, Karen's parents sought the help of another professional, who immediately recommended sending her to a wilderness treatment program. After nearly three months of daily group therapy, backpacking through uninhabited portions of Utah's mountains, and bearing full responsibility for the very basics of life (making her own fire, cooking, cleaning her utensils, pitching a tent to keep dry, washing her few clothes, packing and carrying them to the next campsite, etc.), her counselors decided Karen would benefit from transferring to a therapeutic boarding school. She was not yet ready to return to the environment where she had lost touch with her integrity and sense of her true identity.

The first family visit to Karen's boarding school, after another three months, found her grateful to see her parents. She was scared, though, of how her parents felt about her, how mad they might be, how disgusted. Part of this first visit entailed Karen's honest recounting of her history with drugs and alcohol, sexual activity, and any illegal activities. The blinders came off for everyone, and Karen spiraled into depths of shame she had trouble tolerating. Her counselor wondered whether this would be a time Karen would most like to retreat back into smoking pot. "Yes!" she screamed. "But I can't do that anymore." Her counselor replied calmly and reassuringly, "That's right. You can't go there anymore if you ever expect to discover the real you. But you've cleared the slate with your honesty now, and we can all begin dealing with who you really are." When it became apparent to Karen that her parents still wanted a relationship with her, she fell into their arms. Warmth passed between them for the first time in over a year.

Treatment of Marijuana Dependence

Almost every inpatient treatment program for adolescent chemical dependence is based on what has come to be known as the Minnesota Model, although there are differences in emphasis at different centers. The Minnesota Model emerged in the alcohol field as treatment freed itself from traditional psychiatric medical models that had never proved very helpful. The new idea was a radical departure from Freudian notions of why people became alcoholic. Rather than look for root causes to treat, the Minnesota Model accepted AA's notion that alcoholism is a primary disease, similar to an allergy. From this perspective, treatment focuses on establishing and maintaining abstinence rather than trying to uncover and analyze underlying psychological causes for drinking. Treatment introduces patients to the Twelve Steps through a series of structured assignments and lectures. Psychotherapy and cognitive-behavioral approaches are directed toward removing whatever psychological barriers people have to working these Steps and identifying with the recovering community. In short, treatment supplements the Twelve Step approach with an eye toward eventually enabling patients to remain sober with the support of Twelve Step programs.

On the other hand, some outpatient programs exist today that approach alcoholism very differently—as a bad habit, not a disease. They reject the idea that total abstinence is necessary and offer techniques to teach people controlled drinking. Similarly, some outpatient programs treating drug abuse are guided by a philosophy of harm reduction, which helps people reduce their drug use or switch to the use of less harmful drugs. These two approaches rely more heavily on the use of cognitive-behavioral treatment techniques, using education to change how people think about alcohol and other drug use in order to alter their behavior. They offer an alternative to treatment approaches based on Twelve Step principles.

Nearly all inpatient and the bulk of outpatient treatment programs, however, are either directly based on the Twelve Steps or are careful to remain consistent with this philosophy. Residential programs exist on a continuum ranging from social model centers that rely almost exclusively on introducing patients to Twelve Step programs to medical centers that specialize in what have become known as co-occurring disorders patients—chemical dependents who also suffer from co-occurring psychiatric conditions such as depression, major anxiety, or bipolar disorder.

Because there are variations in emphasis from one treatment center to the next, it is difficult to provide generalizations about the residential treatment that is available for adolescents with marijuana dependence. In most adolescent treatment centers, Twelve Step approaches will play a prominent role. As a result, treatment can be expected to be based on the following principles.

Principles of Drug and Alcohol Treatment

Total Abstinence from Addictive Drugs

Total abstinence from addictive drugs is a mainstay for most treatment programs. People who try to abstain from one drug while using other drugs have not broken the core process of addiction. They are still using chemicals to avoid dealing with emotions. They continue to diminish, rather than nurture, awareness in response to distress. Recovery requires a deep commitment and an unbending intention to stay present and aware.

The scientific basis for encouraging abstinence from *all* drugs of abuse lies within the reward center discussed in chapter 3. All addictive drugs eventually lead to an increase in the brain chemical dopamine within the reward center. Any drug that increases dopamine levels keeps the gateway toward addiction open and well greased. As a result, any drug of abuse can trigger euphoric recall of an addict's original drug of addiction and lead to relapse. Substituting alcohol for marijuana, or marijuana for opiates or cocaine, keeps the reward center from returning to its normal baseline as much as it is able.

Education

Education is a standard part of treatment—education about drugs and how they affect the body and brain, emotions, relationships, and spiritual life. Education about healthy psychological tools for coping with stress is also necessary. Unless people in recovery are able to recognize stress and other triggers for their pot use, relapse becomes likely. Relapse prevention is a critical part of all treatment programs and requires multiple skills, including recognition of emotional states and external triggers for relapse, assertiveness training to resist peer pressure, and cognitive-behavioral skills to convert impulses to use drugs into red flags signaling stress.

Process Groups

Process groups are key to helping people early in abstinence to begin dealing with the continual ebb and flow of emotional energy. Therapy groups operate on two important assumptions. First, shared pain becomes lighter. Living openly and publicly among other recovering people promotes healthy habits. If we are as sick as our secrets, then learning to live openly and vulnerably is the antidote. Second, the power of the group often enables individuals to attempt and accomplish things they could never do alone. Recovery happens in community. Process groups provide the healthiest communities many addicts have ever known, certainly healthier than any they have experienced for quite some time.

Stress Busters

Stress busters are an important part of what has to be learned and practiced in treatment programs. Good nutrition, exercise, sufficient sleep, proper hygiene, and a regular schedule are all part of teaching people how to cope better with stress. In addition, many programs routinely teach stress-reduction techniques such as meditation and yoga, which contribute to maintaining a balanced life. For many adolescents, the discipline of self-care will need to be learned for the first time, which often requires a behaviorally-oriented approach.

Respect, Love, and Hope

Respect, love, and hope are all qualities that treatment programs attempt to wrap around addicts as they gradually emerge from their drug-induced fog. Despite its many flaws, the world is still a beautiful place. Human beings can be the source of much pain to each other, but they can also be benevolent beyond belief. Treatment programs frequently hire addicts and alcoholics with several years of recovery to work closely with patients. Not only do they provide solid role models, but they also respond compassionately to people awakening to the miracle of recovery. The respect, love, and hope they have learned to feel toward themselves flood outward to anyone who is earnestly striving to free himself or herself from addiction.

Recovery

Finally, as previously outlined, treatment programs work to successfully introduce people in early abstinence to recovery. Put succinctly, recovery entails a commitment to achieve more than abstinence. With abstinence alone, people never repair the wreckage of the past that addiction leaves in its wake. This is particularly devastating to adolescents, because this wreckage includes disruptions of their psychological development toward adulthood. Whenever people accept the need for recovery, they are acknowledging the need for fundamental changes if they are ever to live full, rich, and satisfying lives without the aid of drugs and alcohol. The "work" of recovery involves learning a set of tools and practicing their use throughout every day. The slogans ("One day at a time," "First things first," etc.), working with a sponsor, service to others, reading, and meditation need to be incorporated into daily life for recovery to become a reality.

The Unique Needs of Adolescents

Of course, with adolescents there is no fully developed personality to "recover" once abstinence has been achieved. For them, recovery includes working on the process of maturation.

Family Involvement

Family involvement during a child's residential treatment is extremely important if the teen is going to receive the most effective treatment for addiction. This is a time of immense change for the adolescent, and the family often has to change to accommodate the new demands of recovery. In most cases this entails a visit to the treatment center by parents and siblings, although each family's involvement needs to be individualized (for example, in some cases grandparents will also be included; in other cases not all siblings will be included). Many adolescent addicts come from families that were disturbed long before any drug use started, whether overtly or hidden beneath a thick veneer of forced "normality." In either case, family work is valuable for everyone and essential for the adolescent in recovery.

Other families became disturbed primarily when they had to face their youngster's drug use and the escalating misbehavior it produced. Even during peaceful moments, two adults often have difficulty agreeing on drug policies, whether national or within their own home. But to have to come to agreement while already in the midst of an unstable situation involving the child's use is a major challenge. If parents have differences of opinion regarding their child's pot use, their teen will find ways to drive a wedge deeper into the rift, until the parents find themselves focusing on each other rather than the teen. Family counseling is often able to quickly refocus parents on problems that need the most immediate attention—supporting their child's abstinence and creating a healthier home environment that fosters ongoing recovery. Many parents find that they need considerable help in establishing or rebuilding this home environment.

Family involvement is often necessary to support parents through a series of tough decisions they may need to make about what new boundaries and consequences to establish in order to facilitate their teenager's recovery. Tough love often focuses on being tough on children, expecting more responsibility from them than they've shown. But tough love is very tough on parents as well. For example, teens may think they can skate through thirty days of treatment without really doing the work expected of them, only to be confronted by the treatment team's recommendation that their stay be extended for another month or two. In response they look at their parents with a mixture of puppy dog eyes and defiance, and the parents must decide. It takes great restraint to watch children have to experience the consequences of failing to meet a standard that has been set for them. It is difficult to watch children wrestle aimlessly with demons of their own making, rather than to rush in, comfort them, rescue their self-esteem with unbounded parental love, all in part for the parents to feel they are being caring enough. It is tough for parents not to feel *they* have failed somehow when a child fails. Parents need support during their child's treatment for drug addiction to help them make the transition from feeling responsible *for* their child to feeling responsible *to* them. It is not parents' responsibility to make a teen choose sobriety, but it is their responsibility both to make it increasingly uncomfortable for him or her to keep making self-destructive choices and to provide the resources to achieve recovery once the child chooses to move in that direction.

Active Intervention

Active intervention is more frequently required with addicted adolescents because emotional and psychological damage accumulates so much more rapidly during adolescence than during adulthood. If an adult takes five years to gather enough evidence that he or she is being hurt by marijuana use, this is *time* lost, personally and professionally. But if a teen takes five years, basically his or her entire adolescent *development* has been lost. It is far harder to recover from missed development as a teen than it is from missed opportunities as an adult. Without the active participation, and often the initiative, of parents, treatment is far less likely to happen.

Separation from the Using Environment

Separation from the using environment is a standard facet of treatment for both adults and adolescents. A difference often exists, however, between an adult's work environment and a teen's school environment. Many adults can receive adequate treatment while still working because their social network of other drinkers and users is an evening and weekend phenomenon. Intensive outpatient treatment programs that meet evenings and help to structure weekends are often sufficient to separate someone from his or her using friends. Such separation can be more difficult for teens, because the school environment is often where they hang out with other users, buying, selling, and using drugs throughout the day. For this reason, residential treatment that temporarily removes teens completely from their usual environment is frequently warranted and often required.

In a similar vein, many teens find it useful to transfer to smaller charter schools specifically designed to support recovery. For teens, social relationships are intense and generally not balanced by concerns that adults might have (e.g., starting a family or professional development). Helping teens establish relationships with healthy and recovering peers puts them in a strong position to resist any temptation that pulls them back toward their old environments. As a result, residential treatment often requires significant decisions regarding school placement as part of the adolescent's discharge planning, which may necessitate more than the thirty days initially allotted by many insurance plans.

Underlying Issues and Other Psychiatric Problems

Underlying issues and other psychiatric problems such as depression, eating disorders, untreated ADD, or trauma-induced symptoms need to be addressed up front when treating adolescent addiction. When psychiatric conditions have been "self-medicated" by marijuana, it is important to provide effective relief early in abstinence. Medical treatment requires delicate handling. It can confuse a teen who is finally trying to face life without the aid of any chemicals to be given pills to help with facing life.

When adults want to talk a lot about past traumas too early in recovery, they can get distracted from fully accepting their chemical dependence. But the past is not remote for adolescents; childhood is still upon them. Many find that feelings about their parents' divorce, death, abusive behavior, or alcohol or drug addiction—feelings that they submerged with pot—start resurfacing with abstinence. These feelings need to be addressed head-on if teens are ever going to trust that parents are truly concerned with the world as they experience it. Skilled chemical dependence treatment counselors facilitate a recovering teen's reconnection to these buried feelings, treating them as valid and increasing the teen's awareness of how using pot kept them suppressed. Recovery is a time to calculate the cost of using drugs to manipulate one's emotional life.

Developmental Tasks

Developmental tasks that have been aborted by an adolescent's addiction need to be addressed from the very onset of abstinence. In early recovery, most teens feel grossly out of sync with their peers. Emotional maturation is neglected while using, leading teens early in recovery to feel both young and old at the same time, young because they lag behind their peers in emotional and psychological development and old because they have often lost much of the innocence of others their age who have avoided addiction. Teens in early recovery often feel strangely inept without their drug. They may feel too anxious to speak up to a teacher or easily overwhelmed by whatever emotions spring up within them. The only identity they have is that of a stoner and that suddenly is no longer who they are. Rather than finding themselves far ahead of their peers, as they had imagined themselves when using, they now experience themselves as lagging behind, clueless as to how to navigate through the real world successfully. Unless they are quickly guided through neglected developmental tasks, adolescents in early recovery can easily be overwhelmed. To prevent relapse, they need to learn how to accept responsibility for their lives as quickly as possible. The treatment milieu immediately begins the process of holding adolescents accountable for their behavior. An important reason for involving families in treatment is to help parents continue setting the same limits and enforcing the same consequences that their teen responded to in the treatment environment.

Group Therapy

Group therapy is needed to give adolescents an opportunity to connect with peers who are in the same challenging situation. No amount of contact with wise and helpful adults can ever substitute for the value of being with other adolescents in recovery. Discovering that peers have experienced the same doubts and struggles and have the same hopes and longings validates adolescents in ways that no adult ever can. Group therapy provides the arena where adolescents in recovery begin working out the mechanics of healthier relationships.

Structured Environments

Structured environments embody recovery for adolescents. Unlike adults who discontinue using alcohol and other drugs, adolescents can never be exposed to peers with long-term recovery under their belt. By the time teens have several years of successful recovery, they are no longer adolescents. As a result, treatment programs must rely on structured milieus to contain adolescents, all of whom are relatively early in recovery. The structure in residential settings may include prohibiting contact with family except for supervised phone calls in order to decrease the opportunities for pleading to come home and increase a teen's acceptance that he or she is in treatment for the long haul. It may include no contact by phone, mail, or e-mail with friends outside treatment. There is usually a dress code, especially geared to prevent drug-associated messages from contaminating the treatment environment. Little free time is provided, as treatment is not a time for socializing but for serious work. A lot of physical exercise may be part of the structure to provide useful outlets for excess energy as well as to improve physical conditioning, with its positive effect on mood. Many treatment programs are found in remote locations, which decreases the number of runaways without having to resort to locked doors or fences.

Treatment Settings

Treatment services today have been arranged in a hierarchy of ascending intensity, from outpatient to intensive outpatient to day treatment and residential. The greatest number of people are served in settings with the lowest intensity and cost of treatment. Insurance companies are reluctant to authorize higher levels of treatment until an individual has attempted and failed at lower levels, except in more dire emergencies.

Outpatient Treatment

Outpatient treatment programs have greatly expanded during the last decade, largely in response to economic pressures. While the chemical dependence field has lamented the closing of many residential treatment programs, the rise of outpatient treatment has brought some advantages. Outpatient programs have made treatment more widely available by being less expensive and by creating less disruption in people's lives. Outpatient settings also tend to bring treatment into local communities rather than to transport individuals out of their home communities. As a result, outpatient treatment is often more effective in helping people make the transition out of treatment and into community support systems because it connects people with local support from the beginning.

Low-intensity outpatient treatment of adolescents tends to

involve an initial one-on-one evaluation, a weekly counseling meeting, and at least two Twelve Step meetings a week. Some programs primarily provide education, through a structured series of lectures and videos. Others may provide discussion groups. A few run the meetings as ongoing group evaluations, involving all the group members in assessing each other's involvement with alcohol and other drugs. Random urine screens to document sobriety are a part of most outpatient programs.

When adolescents are unable to maintain abstinence with the level of treatment outlined above, they are evaluated for transfer to a higher level of care. In most cases, if their addiction is not life-threatening, they will be referred to an intensive outpatient program or possibly a day treatment setting. Intensive outpatient programs generally last for about three months and require meeting at least three and sometimes five evenings a week. Some group meetings focus on topics, such as presenting one's drug and alcohol history; discussing written exercises that focus on the Steps and tools offered by AA; or stress-reduction techniques. Other groups are process oriented, providing people an opportunity to discuss their struggles and victories in sobriety. The requirement for attending self-help meetings (such as AA or MA or Narcotics Anonymous [NA]) is usually greater in intensive programs, which helps structure weekends. Urine screening is routine.

In effect, three months of an intensive outpatient program provides most of the information and group work that is packed into one month of day treatment or residential programs. Intensive outpatient programs were designed to permit people to continue working and attending school while undergoing treatment.

The essential difference between day treatment (the most intense form of outpatient treatment) and residential treatment is that patients in day treatment leave the program each evening and return home to sleep. Otherwise, they mix with patients in residential treatment and participate in all the same activities. The primary advantages are a decrease in cost and less disruption to one's family.

Residential Treatment

Some teens are compromising their lives by failing school, feeling suicidal, experimenting with other drugs, or being unresponsive to their parents' and counselors' authority, and they need to be lifted out of their current environment if they are going to have a chance at recovery. Residential treatment programs provide an asylum from the outside world and a respite from the stress of daily life that is often necessary for many teens to be able to stop smoking pot. When we remove the opportunity to get high and surround a teen with other adolescents who are struggling with the same problem and with experienced counselors, new things can happen. Counselors can guide the whole community toward recovery through being role models, providing needed education, leading process groups into difficult emotional territory, and creating a safe and hopeful milieu. By surrounding adolescents with a healthy environment twenty-four/seven, we provide them with a vision of what day-to-day life can be when applying the principles of recovery. This vision is not communicated as deeply and clearly in outpatient settings as it is by living recovery for a month or two or more.

Every activity through the day is viewed through the lens of recovery. Cleanliness and promptness are interpreted as issues of respect, for oneself and others in the program. As a result, teens are called on to think in terms of recovery from the moment they wake in the morning. Activities of daily living need to be completed before breakfast, when issues related to proper nutrition are practiced. Mornings usually contain a contemplative exercise, an educational component, time to work on individualized writing assignments, and group therapy. Afternoons usually contain another educational component, physical exercise, individual counseling sessions, time for reading and writing assignments, and group therapy. Community meetings cover issues such as a participant's relapse, bullying or gossip, disrespect, or dishonesty. Evenings are often devoted to a Twelve Step meeting and completing therapy assignments.

While the descent into addiction may have been blindingly swift, the reemergence into sobriety takes time. Many residential treatment programs for adolescents last longer than the twenty-eight days traditionally recommended for adults, primarily because adolescents need to get back onto the developmental path. To accomplish this, treatment programs need to dismantle denial not only about the marijuana addiction but also about developmental issues. Acknowledging that they are immature and have an underdeveloped identity usually delivers quite a blow to teens' fragile pride. They need a supportive environment and skilled guidance to find the path toward maturity. It is best to provide teens enough time in treatment to experience some success and to build up some momentum in recovery before discharging them back into the environment where they first lost their way.

Some arguments against using residential treatment programs include expense and distance from home. After discharge, adolescents return to a community where they don't have a connection to others in recovery. In addition, teens and their families may not have access to aftercare or support from a center located hundreds of miles away. This discontinuity between residential treatment and aftercare is the source of many relapses.

Alternative Settings

Alternative settings have evolved over the past couple of decades. Some programs, based on Outward Bound, use wilderness settings to challenge teens with learning basic survival skills, to introduce them to the power and beauty of nature, and to contain them without requiring locks and keys. Other programs, based on military boot camp models, use rigorous discipline and challenging physical tasks. These models have progressively adopted more sophisticated psychological and therapeutic techniques, and many now not only intervene to protect teens' health and safety but also to begin their treatment.

While some teens enter alternative programs voluntarily, others are delivered to programs by trained and skilled transport services. Typically, parents wake their child at 4:00 A.M., introduce the transport team, instruct their child to do whatever is asked of him or her, and then leave after expressing their love. Such a tactic is a last resort, but it beats standing by impotently and watching their child destroy himself or herself.

Wilderness programs have several valuable qualities. They protect teens' safety by "locking" them into the great outdoors, so far from any town that running away would be nearly impossible. Then, through a combination of physical exercise, intimate exposure to the natural world, constant therapeutic influence, no access to drugs, and being responsible for the most basic functions (e.g., digging latrines, starting a fire with a bow drill, packing and carrying all belongings), recovery begins. The first piece of work is to help teens understand that parents had legitimate reasons to intervene on their behavior. Those participants in wilderness programs who eventually transfer to therapeutic boarding schools will generally be better prepared to enter their placement if they have used the wilderness program to pass through the anger, denial, and acting out that usually follows an intervention.

Wilderness programs can also be of immense value as a booster for recovery. A case in point is a high school student whose parents forced him into treatment early in his senior year. After initially resisting his counselor, he settled into complying with the urine screens and individual and group therapy. The family participated in counseling together. His grades improved substantially. But his parents, who had been attending Al-Anon regularly, had the intuitive sense that a wilderness program during the summer following graduation would still be valuable preparation for their son's entrance into college. He went reluctantly and never truly enjoyed the experience (a city boy through and through). However, with only a couple weeks left in the experience, he decided to get more deeply honest than he had previously been with his parents. He admitted how he had learned to manipulate the results of his urine screens during the outpatient treatment, and although he had cut back his smoking and his grades had improved substantially, he had never been totally clean. He told the truth about how much he had really been smoking before his parents forced him into treatment. And he was able to be far more real with them about the fears he had about being drug-free in college. As a result of his wilderness experience, he decided to live in one of the university's clean and sober dormitories. He is doing extremely well now during his freshman year and credits the deepening of his recovery to whatever happened out there under a night sky filled with stars and solitude.

Posttreatment

Who stays sober? Research indicates that addicts who continue in treatment for a full year tend to achieve long-term sobriety better than those who participate only in an intensive treatment program. For this reason, most programs offer an aftercare program or try to connect graduates with a local aftercare equivalent. In addition to the support provided by weekly aftercare meetings, many adolescents find that they also benefit from transferring to a sober high school. More and more school systems are realizing that sobriety is a difficult lifestyle for teens and requires as much support as possible.

Halfway houses or sober living facilities are also available in some communities. When an adolescent's home environment remains in turmoil, perhaps because a parent is still actively practicing his or her own chemical dependence, a halfway house can be a tremendous support.

Some teens have enough work to do on themselves that they will have a better chance to thrive if they do not return to their home environment but rather move on to a therapeutic boarding school. Usually small and located outside urban areas, therapeutic boarding schools provide age-appropriate academic instruction within a psychologically therapeutic context. Social and emotional growth is pursued as strongly as intellectual progress. Choosing the right therapeutic boarding school for a particular adolescent often requires the help of an educational consultant who is well acquainted with schools across the nation. The topic of therapeutic boarding schools is too large to cover here and is pertinent to only a small fraction of parents with teens addicted to marijuana. Local school counselors and associations of educational consultants (Independent Educational Consultants Association [IECA], www.educationalconsulting.org), wilderness intervention programs, and therapeutic boarding schools (National Association of Therapeutic Schools and Programs [NATSAP], www.natsap.org) are sources of further information.

Insurance

In the past, insurance companies tended to cover residential treatment of chemical dependence as a matter of course. Today most insurance carriers are much more restrictive. Current practices often require an escalating level of treatment intensity, meaning that patients must first be treated in an outpatient setting and fail before payment for inpatient treatment will be authorized.

Once we have become convinced, however, that marijuana or other drug dependence is truly endangering our child's health and safety, it often makes sense to jump to the level of treatment intensity provided only by residential programs and wilderness intervention. As the teen's parents, and presumably the "purchasers/owners" of his or her medical insurance, we are likely to have to advocate on our child's behalf for insurance coverage. An experienced chemical dependence counselor will be an invaluable ally in this fight, especially if the counselor has been working with our teen and can document his or her unwillingness, or unsuccessful efforts, to get clean. Unfortunately, many parents experience an unwillingness by insurance companies to be flexible in responding to their child's crisis. Our best strategy is to swiftly appeal any request that has been turned down, to be persistent, and to remember that the "squeaky wheel" really does get more attention.

Finally, many families do not have any medical insurance. The "squeaky wheel" holds here as well. The local county health and welfare offices can help in navigating through whatever public resources are available. An often forgotten resource is the public school system, which is obligated under law to provide educational opportunities to every child. In some cases, this means funding boarding school for a child for whom the local schools are providing an inadequate educational environment. Schools are not in the business of advertising this option and naturally are resistant to using valuable resources on expensive options for individual students.

The bottom line is clear. Whatever we invest in rescuing a teen sooner rather than later will pay back dividends many times over. Whether we have medical insurance or not, we will likely have to be our child's advocate if we hope to make it sooner.

Chapter 10

Recovery:
Healthy Mind, Body, and Spirit

Recovery is a state of mind that cannot be adequately described in words alone. This fact partly underlies the tradition within Alcoholics Anonymous of "working by attraction, not promotion." We never see advertisements for AA. When I meet people whose lives are firmly committed to recovery, I simply know it. I feel moved by the *freedom, humility, integrity, calm, spirituality, and joy* radiating from their depths. Their recovery is not a fact that I know by logic, but rather by feeling my better nature resonating with them. Recovery opens up our vision and makes us more mindful of reality in all its fullness. Recovery is the antithesis of, and antidote to, addiction—a way of life that is incompatible with getting high or numbing out.

Before Alcoholics Anonymous, drug addiction was generally looked upon as a hopeless condition. The concept of alcoholics' not only regaining their health but then also transforming their lives into profound examples of integrity did not exist. Because the Twelve Step program offered by Alcoholics Anonymous in 1935 was the first avenue to recovery successfully adopted by large numbers of alcoholics, recovery has been closely identified with this tradition. The Twelve Steps have since been adapted to guide a wide array of groups, from Al-Anon to Narcotics Anonymous (NA), Cocaine Anonymous (CA), Overeaters Anonymous (OA), Co-Dependents Anonymous (CODA),

Gamblers Anonymous (GA), and Marijuana Anonymous (MA), to name just a few. The Steps advanced by these programs serve as a record of how the original members of AA found sobriety. The Steps are not prescriptions but suggestions. The genius of AA's program of recovery is that it embodies ancient and universal spiritual truths in a few concrete steps people can grow to understand.[1]

Many people now recognize that the Twelve Steps are an excellent blueprint for anyone wishing to connect more with the depths of their experience, to free themselves from excessive willfulness, to be increasingly realistic about their inherent limitations, to be compassionate, and to open to their spiritual impulses. The Steps are obviously not the only means by which to lead an "examined life," and recovery comes about in a myriad of ways, not only through the Twelve Steps. But they do seem uniquely tailored to facilitate personal growth for those affected by addiction, either directly or by being in a close relationship with an addict. Many family members have joined alcoholics and addicts in recovery.

The Twelve Steps of Marijuana Anonymous* are as follows:

1. We admitted we were powerless over marijuana, that our lives had become unmanageable.
2. Came to believe that a Power greater than ourselves could restore us to sanity.
3. Made a decision to turn our will and our lives over to the care of God, as we understood God.
4. Made a searching and fearless moral inventory of ourselves.
5. Admitted to God, to ourselves, and to another human being the exact nature of our wrongs.
6. Were entirely ready to have God remove all these defects of character.

*Reprinted with permission (see author's note on copyright page).

7. Humbly asked God to remove our shortcomings.

8. Made a list of all persons we had harmed, and became willing to make amends to them all.

9. Made direct amends to such people wherever possible, except when to do so would injure them or others.

10. Continued to take personal inventory and when we were wrong, promptly admitted it.

11. Sought through prayer and meditation to improve our conscious contact with God, as we understood God, praying only for knowledge of God's will for us and the power to carry that out.

12. Having had a spiritual awakening as the result of these steps, we tried to carry this message to marijuana addicts and to practice these principles in all our affairs.

The Characteristics of Recovery

When followed diligently, the Steps introduce people to a state of mind that is characterized by the following:

Freedom

People in recovery finally experience deep freedom from their addiction. The compulsion to use pot to escape rather than tolerate and live through uncomfortable feelings is lifted in recovery. As great a victory as this may sound, it arrives not by overcoming addiction but rather through surrendering to the reality that addiction cannot be overcome but only accepted. Freedom comes from learning which battles to fight and which cannot be won. Freedom comes from accepting realistic limits and from not wasting energy trying to change them. People in recovery are relieved of the need to wage battle with themselves to prove they can use marijuana without losing control.

The paradox of this freedom is that it comes through accepting the need for discipline. Freedom is not license but rather surrender to the fact that not everything in life can possibly be under our control. There are forces far too great to be overpowered, outwitted, or circumvented. Once we accept our limits, including our inability to use drugs without losing control, our energy can be used more effectively.

Humility

Many people flee from recovery because they confuse humility and humiliation. Humiliation is involuntary. It grinds the sense of self-worth out of us and leaves us feeling isolated. Humiliation feels unjust. It feels that something bad has been done to us. And if we accept the humiliation, we end up feeling that we are bad.

Humility, on the other hand, is voluntary. It is a choice to be humble, a choice that many people find difficult. When we are humble, we accept a realistic perspective of ourselves as being quite small in relation to the rest of the universe. When we are humble, we see ourselves as "merely human" and not God, with the full range of human flaws and failings. Humility gives us freedom because it releases us from having to be more than, or different from, who we are. Humility, like freedom, also involves paradox. It requires that we see ourselves as "children of God" while also knowing that "we are not worthy." Humility does not pretend to *understand* such a paradox. It simply accepts it.

Integrity

In Robert Louis Stevenson's story about Dr. Jekyll and Mr. Hyde, the upright doctor ingests a white powder that gives him license to satisfy his every impulse. This story illustrates how addiction *dis*integrates our minds. It drives the different elements of our personality into two camps. We live in one camp when high and in the other camp when straight. There is no integration of the different aspects of our personality—no integrity—when under the influence of a drug.

Marijuana, likewise, diminishes a person's integrity.

Recovery strives to accept all parts of our psychology, the light and the dark, reason and passion, the disciplined parts and the self-indulgent parts that lie within each of us. Integrity begins with rigorous honesty, always accepting the truth about what we are thinking and feeling. Integrity also demands that we square our behavior with our values and that we truly measure our own behavior by the same yardstick used to measure others. When a person has committed himself or herself to recovery, what you see is what you get.

Calm

Calm, or serenity, is a hallmark of recovery. As addiction splits the personality into separate camps, people begin to be at war with themselves. Their lives are overtaken by the drama of this internal conflict. The deeper people sink into addiction, the higher the highs and the lower the lows they feel. With recovery comes balance and with balance comes calm.

Recovery calms people by eliminating unnecessary drama from their lives. For example, the bottom line of remaining sober ("First things first") keeps day-to-day events in perspective, and the habit of pausing to think before reacting moderates responses to perceived insults and slights. An important, calming change also occurs when people begin to seek depth in their emotional lives, as opposed to the intensity they sought during active addiction. Still waters run deep, unlike the tumultuous white water of shallow rapids.

Spirituality

The foundation of serenity in recovery is a reinvigoration of one's spiritual life. Many people come to believe during recovery that a deep and aching spiritual emptiness was an important motivator for their alcohol and other drug use. This does not mean an absence of religion, but rather a lack of connection to the universe and the profundity of experience within. This is spiritual bankruptcy—separation from the rest of life and from sources of vitality other than our own willpower.

The impulse to connect to a greater whole is nearly universal in humans, giving rise to a sense of awe and mystery since the dawn of our species. Connecting with forces that are much greater than ourselves has the power to reawaken the whole of who we are. The pursuit of these connections is the essence of the spiritual journey. Recovering people accept the spiritual needs that lie within them, nurture awareness of them, and work to stay as open as possible to how those needs might be met, whether through solitude, meditation, prayer, church, nature, or support groups. The means of reconnecting with the infinite are infinite. We can tell others the way that has worked for us, but each must find his or her own.

Joy

Sobriety may be serious business, but it is not somber. Laughter is a frequent guest at Twelve Step meetings. Recovery aims to create a full, rich, and satisfying life, without the illusions provided by drugs and alcohol. People in recovery from marijuana learn that, while pot made a lot of things seem funny, it never led to any lasting joy. Recovery teaches that laughter, giggling, hilarity, giddiness, silliness, humor, and the ridiculous are available to the straight world, too. And people tend to remember the good times better!

Can all these qualities of recovery really be understood and practiced by adolescents? Yes. I have seen so many young people successfully rebuild their lives on the principles of recovery that I have no reservations answering in the affirmative. We do a disservice if we underestimate the ability of a teen to grab onto recovery with tenacity and deep intention.

Levels of Recovery

Just as addiction develops over time, evolving through a series of levels, so does recovery. As adolescents move deeper into recovery, we can expect them to reach three important levels.

Recovery of Abstinence

The first level of recovery from marijuana dependence is a cleansing. As the brain is detoxified from the chronic imbalance forced on its endocannabinoid system by THC, mental clarity is recovered. This can take weeks and perhaps even months, as THC stored in the rest of the body is gradually released and excreted. Because the endocannabinoid system influences the brain's sensitivity to a host of other neurotransmitters, the normal biochemical ecology has to reestablish itself gradually. Like a forest regrowing after a fire, full mental clarity takes time to develop and mature.

A cleansing process has to take place psychologically as well. Denial is a mental toxin. By the time most people enter recovery, they have usually been in denial for years to protect their smoking. Recovery requires that they hunt down denial wherever it has lodged in their minds and dissolve it with the light of day. Honesty is the antidote for denial. It can scrub minds clean if practiced rigorously.

Most people also need to clean up their relationships after getting into recovery. The main contaminant that marijuana imports into relationships is an addict's unwillingness to own responsibility for his or her behavior. Addicts blame. They blame others for causing their own misbehavior. They blame the injustice of the world for their indiscretions. They blame fate for their failures. Recovery eventually demands that we all take responsibility for our own actions, our own thoughts, and our own feelings. We do not determine everything that happens to us, but we are ultimately responsible for how we react to the events of our lives.

Recovery of Psychological Growth

Another level of recovery is reached when abstinence kick-starts the maturation process into motion again. Smoking marijuana creates a beguiling illusion of being grown up even as it can slow, and then stop, normal development. Unlike adults who fell away from maturation when addiction arrived, adolescents have no mature identity to recover. Adolescents need to recover the normal drives that motivate psychological growth.

For many, restarting the maturation process begins with *accepting the identity of being an addict* and then moving beyond it. Just as each of us is a male or a female but more than just male or female, adolescents recovering from marijuana dependence need to accept being an addict as a central part—but only a *part*—of their identity. This acceptance nails down an honest assessment of what happened in their relationship to marijuana, i.e., loss of control. Accepting one's identity as an addict permanently works against the natural impulse to reestablish denial, and it provides the humility to accept that life had gotten off track and that help is needed to get going again. The fault for having been derailed from the normal path of adolescent development lies in the addiction. The reason teen addicts lag behind their peers in accomplishing age-appropriate developmental tasks is the impact marijuana has had on their brains. Once pot is removed and its effects repaired, adolescents are free to venture into adulthood. This is freedom.

Recovering a sense of community is also vital to further psychological growth. Perhaps the most damaging punishment is to be shunned, to be excluded by one's home community. Most addicts have been misunderstood and judged, and many believe they *deserve* to be shunned. The shame of having violated their own values and the core values of their home (both family and tribe) leaves many addicts feeling cut off, like outcasts. There is, fortunately, one community that recovering addicts fully qualify for—the community of other recovering addicts. Reentry into full membership in the human race often begins by identifying with other adolescents in recovery. This is a place where adolescents can begin to feel a deep sense of belonging again. This is critical, because the experience of addiction ultimately robs people of any sense of legitimacy and acceptability to others.

By joining the recovering community, adolescents include themselves in a vital set of relationships with people who have successfully passed through the "dark side of life." They model the kind of freedom, humility, integrity, calm, spirituality, and joy that we would all hope our children see as goals they can reach.

Recovering wholeness is also necessary for adolescents. If marijuana *dis*integrates the personality, recovery *re*integrates it. The Twelve Steps provide principles that allow people to achieve far more than abstinence (although they are excellent tools for achieving that bottom-line goal, too). The principles can also be married to the whole of our psychological growth. Whatever changes are required of teens as they mature are made easier by a clear understanding of their limitations, an honest assessment of their strengths, and an open reliance on the help of others. Recovery pursues emotional wholeness as an achievable goal, although it reminds all of us that while progress toward that goal is possible, perfection is not.

Recovery of Meaning and Purpose

Because marijuana dependence harms the body, mind, and spirit, recovery must address all three levels. The third level of recovery involves healing the spirit, which is necessary for developing a mature sense of meaning and purpose. Few young children are worried about what life means or what their reason for living might be. But this becomes a central theme for most adolescents, who have serious questions about purpose and meaning.

When the drug-induced sense of awe and wonder that comes from flooding the amygdala with THC substitutes for spiritual connection, the source of mystery is located outside, in the material world, rather than in the inner self: *"Smoke this joint and you can find God."* For some, the chemical sense of wonder awakens a desire for greater spiritual connection. But for many, the words of Alan Watts sum up the danger of this chemical trap: "The common error . . . is . . . to look at the finger pointing the way and then to suck it for comfort rather than follow it." In the case of marijuana dependence, sucking on the joint is a substitute for seeking a more substantial spiritual calling.

When addicts recover access to their whole being and are honest about what they find within, they usually discover long-neglected or denied spiritual needs. While many adolescents may want to ignore these needs, the integrity that develops during recovery demands that people develop a willingness to deal with *all* of their feelings—pleasant, unpleasant, and awkward. The Twelve Steps work in part because they provide a spiritual program that addresses this longing.

Faith is a kind of knowing that stems from neither reason nor evidence. Faith requires a willingness to believe and trust in something other than ourselves, something that is not under our direction or control. Faith does not require a belief in God. It may be faith in our body's, or the earth's, ability to heal itself. It may be faith in the wisdom of our unconscious or intuition. It may be faith in the collective actions and generosity of other people. Or it may be faith in the forces guiding the universe, whether we call this God or not. Spirituality begins when we are willing to look outside our usual sense of self and accept that other powerful forces influence our lives.

Not everybody finds the same Higher Power influencing their lives, and not everyone calls it by the same name. Some may call it their Buddha nature, others call it God, Yahweh, Allah, or even the collective unconscious. But, while not everyone accepts having the same Higher Power, most people in recovery accept that there is a power greater than themselves. They may feel this Higher Power through the recovering community, nature, or direct contact with the God of their understanding. Whatever an addict understands his or her Higher Power to be, coming into deeper relationship with it is an important level of recovery. Paradoxically, voluntarily surrendering to it is a source of freedom. That which meets our spiritual needs helps us move from groping for meaning and purpose to a place of true belonging.

Chapter 11

Prevention:
Philosophies and Protective Factors

Even if the majority of people who have used marijuana never experience overt difficulties, preventing the minority of people who do become dependent from having to experience the havoc that addiction brings to their lives is worthwhile. The personal suffering of adolescents whose lives are affected well into adulthood by the early onset of marijuana dependence is enormous, as is the impact that their difficulties have on their families and their communities' educational, judicial, and social welfare resources. From both a public health standpoint and a position of basic human compassion, prevention of such suffering and disruption is an important goal.

Because the percentage of people who become harmfully involved with pot rises steadily with decreasing age of initiating use, prevention efforts are most appropriately directed toward minors. People who begin using marijuana as adolescents are at greatest risk, so adolescents should receive the most attention. The greatest benefit prevention efforts could produce would be to contribute to adolescents *avoiding* or at least *delaying* trying pot.

Powerful barriers work against success in the prevention arena, not the least of which is the difficulty of proving that anything works. The subculture of adolescence is a moving target, changing and morphing by the minute. Researchers can neither hope to account for all the shifting variables that mold adolescent attitudes and behavior nor hope to predict the politics that determine which prevention strategies will be funded and how their results will be translated into policy. The Reagan era's "Just say no" campaign, for example, arose more from a political philosophy than from public health research, yet it dominated prevention efforts for nearly a decade. Even when a prevention strategy *does* appear to influence some individuals positively, it is difficult to prove beyond a doubt that the intervention was the critical factor in producing the change.

What to Prevent?

Theoretical problems confronting the prevention field run deep. The public, and even prevention experts themselves, can rarely agree on exactly *what* we should be trying to prevent. Should we be trying to prevent *all* use of marijuana or just abuse and dependence? This divergence in perspectives has far-reaching consequences.

Those who would strive to prevent all marijuana use fall into the "prohibitionist" camp. They are more inclined to adopt strategies designed to control the available supply of marijuana, usually both to teens and adults. They see all use of pot as being misuse. The more militant contingent among prohibitionists tends to favor stricter laws, tighter borders, and greater funding for law enforcement.

Those who aim to diminish the harm marijuana does to some people, that is, to prevent abuse and dependence, fall into the *harm reduction*, or *responsible use*, camp. They are more inclined to adopt strategies that educate and provide access to treatment. The more militant among the harm reductionists and responsible-use advocates champion legalization of marijuana. (This debate is explored further in chapter 12).

If experts and local communities cannot agree on what to prevent, it becomes difficult for school districts to develop a unified strategy for funding and implementing effective prevention programs. Even when researchers are able to create programs that demonstrate some success in preventing or delaying adolescent drug use, schools may not have the resources to purchase them. As a result, America has no coherent and rational drug prevention strategy in place today.

No Guarantee

I have more compelling, personal reasons for feeling cautious about our ability to prevent *either* all use of marijuana *or* its problematic use. I have seen scores of teenagers, including my own, hurt by their marijuana use even though they received some of the most thorough prevention education available. Imagine our friends' consternation and concern: both my wife and I are therapists, with training and experience in the field of addictions. We have been active in local schools helping to design and deliver alcohol and drug education. Many acquaintances feel we qualify as poster children for how scary it is to be raising a teenager. If *we* couldn't prevent problems in our home despite our familiarity with addiction, what chance do parents without training in the field have to safeguard their children?

The truth is that our prevention efforts could not guarantee that our daughter would not experiment with marijuana. We did the best we could to delay her use, but the choice was ultimately up to her, as it is with every teen. And we could not have prevented her from being attracted to the mood swing once she had experienced marijuana.

While we couldn't prevent her use, we did intervene with the swiftness of greased lightning. While we did not prevent the initial harm that marijuana dependence produced, we did reduce the damage considerably by removing her from the environment where her behavior was out of control. We did interrupt her use long enough for her to be introduced to a clear head and the program of recovery. Once we had led her forcibly to the trough of recovery, we could not make her drink.

But recovery is eventually attractive to many people in ways that pot can never be. Pot can beguile and seduce. Recovery can liberate and enrich. To a clear mind, the choice between the two is easy.

Different Needs

Prevention is also complicated by the fact that, despite having many developmental issues in common, adolescents vary greatly. Every school has teens who will never try pot or other drugs. For other teens, it will truly be experimentation—a few trials to see what the experience is all about. Prevention for these two groups means nothing more than making sure honest information is available.

At the other end of the spectrum is the group that is bound to use, and probably abuse, marijuana no matter what prevention efforts are targeted on them. For this group, prevention consists of educating the teens about recovery as an eventual possibility, as well as supporting parents to intervene. The goal is to prevent as much long-term damage as possible.

It is the broad middle group of teens—those between the group that needs little or no prevention education to avoid using marijuana and the group that is impervious to prevention efforts—who will benefit most from the avoid-or-delay message. They represent the middle of a bell-shaped curve and are both the easiest to influence and the most likely to modify their behavior on the basis of reliable information.

Facts versus Fear

While drug education is most likely to affect the middle group of students, it fails them when it relies on fear tactics. On the one hand, proponents of prohibition may emphasize the dangers of marijuana use beyond what the facts warrant, primarily out of a motivation to protect kids. On the other hand, proponents of responsible use may denigrate being cautious about pot, also beyond what the facts warrant.

Between fear tactics about marijuana and denial of the realistic dangers that do exist for some adolescents lies an honest presentation of the facts. Use equals risk. Risk is not equally distributed. It is at least as normal not to experiment with marijuana as it is to try it. Among those who first use marijuana at age eighteen or older, approximately 10 percent eventually become dependent. The younger use begins, the greater the risk of addiction. These are the facts, and we need to rely on adolescents to use these facts to make healthy choices. Efforts to inflame their fear inevitably backfire. Once teens realize we have manipulated the truth, they are unlikely to believe anything else we tell them, even the facts. Once again, integrity is essential if we want teens to listen.

The facts about how THC affects our brains by mimicking a natural neurotransmitter fall nicely in between the War on Drugs and the Helium Balloon models. The War on Drugs is a framework for viewing marijuana advanced by many prohibitionists. Originally arising from President Richard Nixon's perspective that drugs are evil and drug users are bad, irresponsible people who threaten the fabric of American society, this framework oozes fear. It posits evil in a plant and gives the commandment to "just say no" to eating the forbidden fruit. This moralistic view implies that drug users are immoral. What is a fourteen-year-old to conclude when he or she takes a couple tokes from a joint in a friend's bedroom and giggles for a few hours? Has this teen suddenly become Satan? He or she knows the next morning that he or she is no more evil than ever before, no more immoral than before experimenting. The natural conclusion is that the War on Drugs is some massive manipulation by grown-ups. In fact, it probably *is* largely a manipulation of the electorate by certain politicians. Propaganda will never work as a primary prevention strategy. It is based on fear and manipulation and lacks integrity.

The Helium Balloon is a framework for viewing marijuana advanced by those interested in its legalization. Perhaps first popularized by the hippie movement of the late sixties and early seventies, this perspective holds that marijuana is essentially as harmless as helium, an inert gas inhaled from a balloon that magically and temporarily makes us all talk like Donald Duck. Hilarious. How could a little party trick ever be evil incarnate? And, since laughter is good for what ails us, it probably even has healing powers for the soul as well.

The facts are neutral and fall in between these two popular extremes. They do not support any political or social philosophy. They support only the truth. And providing the truth supports adolescents' growth into discerning, intelligent adults.

External Protective Factors

Despite the difficulties in designing drug prevention programs, there are identifiable factors, external and internal, that do protect adolescents' health in the face of a world filled with drugs. Being aware of these protective factors permits parents to work to strengthen them whenever possible.

The primary external protective factor stems from *community willingness* to expand drug prevention efforts beyond the school-based programs that are generally employed. Too often a school district surveys available drug prevention curricula and then chooses and implements one without any community input. As a result, drug education gets nicely contained as an adolescent problem, to be dealt with not by the community as a whole but by paid educators in the classroom. Clearly there is a role for school participation in efforts to protect teens' drug health, but the programs that have demonstrated the biggest benefit have generally been far more community based.

One example of a community-based prevention program is Project Northland,[1] undertaken in the early nineties in twenty-four school districts and twenty-eight adjoining Minnesota communities. The project coordinated efforts in the school curricula, parental involvement programs, extracurricular peer leadership programs, and other community mobilization strategies. The target group studied was students in sixth to eighth grades. The results of this community-based approach were significant. Eighth graders who had completed three years of the program had a 46 percent decrease in weekly alcohol use compared with control groups. Marijuana use was down 50 percent and cigarette use was down 37 percent. Researchers analyzing the data concluded that the program was considerably more effective with students who had not yet started any alcohol or drug use before the sixth grade. In other words, Project Northland was better at delaying use than at reducing use among those who had already started. Perhaps this reflects the fact that it is the large middle group of youngsters who are most capable of being influenced, not those at either end of the continuum who have already committed themselves to using or to abstaining.

Drug addiction is hardly a problem confined to the adolescent years. It is a social problem that has been described as an "equal opportunity destroyer." Every segment of every community contains individuals whose lives are being eroded and destroyed by alcohol and other drugs. Communities that are willing to look at themselves and not shine the light of attention only on teenagers are far more likely to create a healthy atmosphere for growing up. Communities that are willing to discuss their values and norms regarding marijuana, to recognize and respect diversity in perspectives, and thereby to foster open and direct communication among parents, are going to model for their children how to weed denial out of the picture when confronting difficult issues.

Another external protective factor is the level of *emotional safety in the school environment*. My wife and I organized a Drug and Alcohol

Advisory Committee at our local middle school for several years. We accomplished a few things—improved funding for drug education, surveyed students about their patterns of use and attitudes about drugs and alcohol, and forged an alliance between a local adolescent treatment program and the school. But we never affected the community as a whole. We never ignited that spark needed to lead drug education out of being anything more than an add-on to the school curriculum.

Eventually we came to realize that we were trying to create an island of safety in a shark-infested sea. Our drug education program was trying to move beyond merely repeating the facts about drugs. We were encouraging kids to talk openly and honestly about how they thought about alcohol and other drugs, to speak about their personal values and experiences, and to expose themselves to scrutiny and possible judgment by others. If the parents thought it was too dangerous to be so vulnerable, their children were certainly not going to feel any freer.

We began to see how a school community that tolerates harassment, put-downs, bullying, and disrespect among students without being aware of the extent to which these social toxins permeate their children's world (and we live in a polite, upscale suburban community) is impervious to effective exploration of its attitudes about mind-altering chemicals. Alcohol and drug prevention programs will probably enjoy their greatest success in schools that embed this education in a wider program teaching social and emotional competence.

An effective drug prevention strategy cannot lie within the narrow arena traditionally considered as drug education. Kids get the facts about drugs, and they generally get the facts over and over. What most of them don't get is the social and emotional learning necessary to understand and integrate the facts. Most students don't get training in how to relate to each other with the respect and integrity necessary to develop an atmosphere conducive to honest communication. Kids are more likely to behave appropriately with drugs if their school does not tolerate inappropriate behavior in general.

As a result, our local middle school now has a Social/Emotional Safety Committee, with drug education as one topic alongside issues of sexual harassment, body image, anger management, conflict resolution, and violence. Unless schools foster an atmosphere of *deep safety*—and unless that atmosphere is valued throughout the school community— the effect of its drug prevention program will remain limited.

Internal Protective Factors: Resiliency

In describing characteristics that put a teen at increased risk of marijuana abuse, I listed not only underlying psychiatric issues such as ADD, depression, and suffering from trauma but also personality traits such as a penchant for taking risks and an attraction to excitement. On the other hand, certain personality traits can *protect* individuals from being easily knocked off course by drugs. These are inherent characteristics that lead individuals to be resilient in the face of stresses. Such resilience decreases the attraction marijuana might have as a means for coping with turmoil.

Steven and Sybil Wolin provide a useful summary of resiliency factors in *The Resilient Self*. Following are the seven resiliencies they identify:

- insight: the habit of asking tough questions and giving honest answers
- independence: drawing boundaries between yourself and others
- relationships: having intimate and fulfilling ties to other people that balance a mature regard for your own needs with empathy and the capacity to give to someone else
- initiative: taking charge of problems, exerting control, having a taste for stretching and testing yourself in demanding tasks

- creativity: imposing order, beauty, and purpose on the chaos of troubling experiences and painful feelings
- humor: finding the comic in the tragic
- morality: having an informed conscience that extends your wish for a good personal life to all of humankind

It's unlikely that any child possesses the full range of resiliency characteristics, but the full range is not needed. Most teens possess some of these characteristics, in some measure. As parents and educators, we have a greater chance of strengthening the resources each child already possesses than of teaching them perspectives and skills that they do not yet possess. For example, one child might cope well with distress by using his or her intellect, eventually containing any turmoil in a protective coating of understanding. Another child in the same family may deal with similar feelings better by picking up crayons and drawing a picture that contains the emotion. Helping the first child ask more probing questions and find more honest answers will be more useful than putting a crayon in his or her hand. And hanging the second child's drawing on the refrigerator, in a place of honor, and encouraging that child to keep drawing may help more than making him or her sit and explain what he or she is feeling verbally. When we help children develop whatever natural talents they have for coping with stress, we make them more resilient.

A Neglected Answer: Student Assistance Programs

Because the risk of marijuana and other drug dependence is not evenly distributed, prevention efforts need to be individualized more than standardized curricula permit. Information that may be critical for teens debating with themselves about whether to try marijuana may be old hat to students who have been smoking for a year already. The disdain that marijuana-savvy students often feel for others who are more naive quickly stifles open dialogue. Also, some information is just too private and personal to be discussed in front of other students. For example, it is often too risky for a teen to speak out about his or her concern that an older sister's pot smoking is getting out of control or that his or her mother has to be put to bed every night because she's passed out drunk on the floor. Some things are so sensitive that kids are reluctant to tell a teacher, especially if the teacher is already frustrated with them for not performing up to their potential. The bottom line is that teens often need the same level of confidentiality as adults do to deal with sensitive problems.

Many adults have access to employee assistance programs (EAPs) for psychological help. EAPs are designed to give adults easy access to emotional support that is completely divorced from their direct work environment. The logic behind EAPs is that people are naturally reluctant to speak personally to supervisors who have responsibility for evaluating their job performance and recommending raises and promotions. Many businesses have therefore provided a separate, entirely confidential track to provide employees support for personal issues. By providing confidential EAP services, people are able to receive the individualized help they need, when they need it.

A few schools have realized the confidentiality needs of children, although their place of "employment" is the school. By teaming up with local community mental health centers, these schools have developed student assistance programs (SAPs)—confidential, on-site support services for teens. SAPs have discovered that the majority of students seeking their services are somehow involved with alcohol and other drugs. Students living with addicted parents flock to student assistance programs. Students concerned with their own drug use, or with a friend's or older sibling's use, make appointments. Students too depressed to perform well in school often end up dealing with their drug use at SAPs. The safety net that student assistance programs throw under a school community is wide and catches many problems resulting from alcohol and other drugs. The individual services this net can provide makes it one of the most effective drug prevention strategies any community can develop.

A Message to Adolescents

I end this chapter with thoughts from Andrew Weil, author of *The Natural Mind* and *From Chocolate to Morphine*. They offer the best-worded cautionary message to adolescents about drug use that I have ever seen.

> To our teen-age readers we offer some general advice at the start:
>
> You are growing up in a world well stocked with drugs. All of them can be used wisely or stupidly. Grownups will give you much misinformation about them and will often be dishonest or hypocritical about their own drug use. You will see many of your acquaintances become involved with drugs and will have many opportunities to experiment with them yourself if you have not already done so. The fact that grownups exaggerate the dangers of drugs they disapprove of does not mean those drugs have no dangers. All drugs are dangerous.
>
> The only way you can be absolutely sure of avoiding problems with drugs is never to use them. This is a perfectly reasonable choice and may allow you more freedom than your drug-taking peers. You may feel left out of certain groups if you abstain, but you will not really be missing anything. All of the experiences people have with drugs can be had in other ways. If you do decide to experiment with drugs, whether approved or disap-

proved, make sure you know what the drugs are, where they come from, how they are likely to affect your body, and what precautions you should take to contain their potential for harm. Remember that forming good relationships with drugs is not easy, and maintaining them takes work. Don't use drugs unconsciously and don't spend time around people who do.

If you are tempted to experiment with illegal drugs, keep in mind that being arrested can bring terrible consequences to you and your family. On the other hand, do not make the mistake of supposing that just because a drug is legal it is safe. Some of the strongest and most dangerous drugs are legal. . . .

It is a bad idea to take drugs in school. Even if school bores you, you have to be there, and mastering classroom skills is your ticket to freedom and independence in adult life. Drugs can interfere with your education by making it hard to pay attention, concentrate, and remember, or by involving you with people who reinforce negative attitudes about school.

Drugs are likely to be a source of friction between you and your parents. If your parents get upset with you for taking drugs, consider that they might have good reasons, such as valid fears about your safety, health, or psychological growth. Be willing to talk honestly with them and to hear their side with an open mind. Think about how you would feel in their place. What advice would you give your child if you found out he was taking drugs? Question your parents about the drugs they use. Maybe they will agree to give up theirs if you will give up yours. Try to see what your experiences have in common with theirs. What alternatives to drug use can your parents suggest? If you can convince them that your drug use is responsible, you may be able to allay their anxiety. If their fears come from ignorance or misinformation, try to educate them, not by being emotional but by being well informed about the drugs you use. . . .

Finally, remember that wanting to change your consciousness is not a symptom of mental illness or an unhealthy need to escape from reality. It is normal to want to vary your conscious experience. Drugs are just one way of doing it, though, and if you come to rely on them before you are grown up, you may not be able to appreciate a whole range of nondrug experiences that are more subtle but more rewarding over time. There is no question that drugs get you high, but they are difficult to master and will fail you if you take them too often. . . .[2]

The chief advantage of drugs is that they are quick and effective, producing desired results without requiring effort. Their chief disadvantage is that they fail us over time; used regularly and frequently, they do not maintain the experiences sought and, instead, limit our options and freedom.[3]

Once people get into bad relationships with drugs it is very hard to get them out. For most abusers the only practical choice is total abstinence or continued abuse. (Italics added)[4]

Chapter 12

Current Debates about Marijuana:
Cutting through the Rhetoric

American opinion is currently divided on two core issues regarding marijuana: (1) Should marijuana be legalized, and (2) is there a legitimate role for the medical use of marijuana? Most public debate about these issues has been extremely polarized, producing frequent high-profile news items. As adamant as voices from each camp can be, their viewpoints usually leave out some important considerations.

Current debates about marijuana constitute part of the environment within which adolescents make their decisions regarding whether to smoke pot or not. Those who do use marijuana often become well versed in arguments favoring its legalization and medical use in an effort to rationalize their smoking. In this chapter, we're going to look beyond the standard arguments and address important considerations usually left out of the debates.

A Brief History of America's War on Drugs

It is nearly impossible to explain the polarized viewpoints people have about marijuana without first looking at the War on Drugs. Prior to 1967, the federal government had little involvement in drug enforcement. That year, Richard Nixon and congressional Republicans were criticizing President Lyndon Johnson for being soft on crime in light of domestic disturbances arising from opposition to the Vietnam War and from deep racial inequities brought into national awareness by the Civil Rights movement. In response, Johnson began the trend that culminated in our national War on Drugs. He took regulatory powers away from the Food and Drug Administration (FDA) and created within the Department of Justice the Bureau of Narcotics and Dangerous Drugs (BNDD), the predecessor of today's Drug Enforcement Administration (DEA). With this change, the researchers and scientists at the FDA were no longer in control of drug policies; federal police and legal prosecutors had become responsible for setting drug policy. Doctors no longer controlled the assessment of a drug's potential danger.

As Johnson decided not to seek reelection, Richard Nixon was developing a strong law-and-order platform. In October 1967 he wrote in a *Reader's Digest* article, "The country should stop looking for the 'root causes' of crime and put its money instead into increasing the number of police."[1] By the time the 1968 presidential campaign was in full swing, Nixon put the capstone on his law-and-order theme by pronouncing drugs to be the "curse of the youth, just like the plagues and epidemics of former years. And they are decimating a generation of Americans." He promised that his administration would "accelerate the development of tools and weapons"[2] to fight crime by fighting illegal drugs. The War on Drugs had been invented as a campaign theme based on fear, and a majority of Americans made it a winning strategy. (A fascinating in-depth history of America's War on Drugs can be found in Dan Baum's *Smoke and Mirrors: The War on Drugs and The Politics of Failure*.)

Marijuana was a perfect political symbol for focusing people's fear and anger at a counterculture that was threatening to abandon American values. Compounding misperceptions that stemmed from political fear-mongering was the fact that Americans tended to lump all illegal drugs together. Little distinction was made between heroin and pot, even in articles appearing in mainstream magazines such as *Newsweek, Life,* and *Time.* The dangers of marijuana were portrayed out of proportion to its actual significance as a public health hazard (e.g., more Americans died falling down stairs in 1969 than from using all illegal drugs, and none died from pot). At the same time, the concept of addiction as a disease with origins in the brain was not yet thoroughly established within the scientific community. Much of the public still subscribed to Richard Nixon's repudiation of "root causes," believing that crime and drug use reflected the character of those involved and was not a reflection of society as a whole. The War on Drugs was more a politically motivated war against "bad" people who chose to be drug addicts and criminals than it was a well-thought-out public health policy.

Decades later, we are still affected by the legacy of the War on Drugs, despite ample evidence of its failure and abuses. One of the best summaries of this legacy is portrayed by the movie *Traffic,* in which the president's nominee for drug czar is so disheartened by the prospect of continuing bankrupt policies from the past that he resigns before even taking office. He explains plaintively, "A war against drug users is a war against ourselves." The legacy of this war is a harvest of bitterness, social injustice, and hypocrisy that has contributed to polarizing American society to a point beyond meaningful dialogue. It is in this unhealthy atmosphere, created and maintained in large part by the War on Drugs, that adolescents make their decisions regarding whether to smoke pot.

Incarceration and the War on Drugs

Marijuana is an illegal drug in the United States; people who grow or possess it are breaking the law. That is the reality. The reality is also that laws banning marijuana are broken almost as frequently as speed limits and the IRS tax code. In cases that flagrantly violate the law and cause harm to others, such as dealing pot or causing a serious accident, the general agreement is that punishment is warranted. It is in the lesser offenses that incarceration may do more harm than good. America's predilection for punishing marijuana users through incarceration has existed long enough for us to review the consequences.

The War on Drugs has led to an unprecedented increase in America's prison population. Since the 1970s, incarceration has been our primary drug prevention strategy. FBI Uniform Crime Reports indicate that of the 1.1 million arrests in the United States in 1990, approximately one-quarter were for marijuana possession. By 1995 the number of marijuana arrests had doubled to more than half a million, with 86 percent being for possession. In 2000, 46.5 percent of the total arrests for drug violations—734,497—were for marijuana. Of these, 646,042 were arrests for possession alone. Depending on the state, as many as one-third of those arrested for possessing marijuana were incarcerated. From 1980 to 1997, the number of people entering prison for violent offenses doubled, while nonviolent offenses tripled and drug offenses increased *elevenfold.*

The imprisonment of marijuana users sometimes creates a level of harm to people's lives that may equal or exceed that produced by marijuana smoking itself. Lives are disrupted, young people are placed in cells with more serious criminals, and felony records haunt them for years. People with serious addictions are punished rather than treated. The racial imbalance of law enforcement has alienated whole communities. Most drug-related arrests of ethnic minorities involve possession of marijuana for personal use. Even Richard Nixon's Presidential Commission unexpectedly came to the conclusion in 1972 that the harm of an arrest was significantly greater than the harm from using marijuana. At the same time, there is no convincing evidence that imprisonment has diminished either the supply of marijuana or the number of marijuana smokers.

Imprisonment fails society on several levels. If an individual is truly addicted to marijuana, incarceration is a poor substitute for treatment and could be likened to quarantining a tuberculosis patient without providing medical care. Forced abstinence is a punishment that rarely leads to recovery by itself, although many prisons today are now offering drug treatment as an avenue for early release. On the other hand, individuals not addicted but guilty of possessing marijuana sit in prison while those whose drug of choice is alcohol are permitted to sit in bars.

There are tremendous racial disparities in the enforcement of drug laws. By 1986 the nation's prisons held more blacks than whites, although blacks make up only 12 percent of the general population.[3] Between 1985 and 1987, 99 percent of all drug-trafficking defendants nationwide were African American. In 1989, 35 percent of all African American males between sixteen and thirty-five were arrested, a figure that illustrates the profound impact that law enforcement has had on the black population. Although African Americans and Hispanic Americans constitute only 20 percent of marijuana users in the United States, 58 percent of those sentenced under federal law in 1995 for marijuana offenses were from those two ethnic groups. From 1986 to 1996, the number of young whites incarcerated for drug offenses rose by 90 percent, while the number of young blacks rose by 539 percent.

Different states show remarkable disparity in the penalties they levy for the possession of marijuana for personal use. For example, while ten states have a maximum sentence of five years or less, just as many states have a maximum penalty of thirty years or more. Under federal law, the punishment for possessing a single joint has been the same as for possessing small amounts of heroin, cocaine, or crack.

The progressive intensification of law enforcement to solve America's problem with drug abuse eventually led to a harsh disregard for civil liberties, such as having personal property seized and sold upon being arrested for drug possession (under RICO, the Racketeering Influenced and Corrupt Organizations Act), without a trial ever having to be conducted. In 1991, 80 percent of people who had property confiscated were never charged with a crime. Even when a trial finds a defendant not guilty, it is often impossible to reclaim seized property. While such tactics were originally developed to combat organized crime, they became an important source of revenue for the War on Drugs. In 1991, half a billion dollars was seized by the Justice Department, with much of this used to support law enforcement and the construction of prisons.

The expense of incarceration is put into perspective by looking at the comparison of annual costs for responding to an addict in a variety of ways. For example, in 1997 regular outpatient treatment cost $1,800, while intensive outpatient treatment cost $2,500. Methadone maintenance of heroin addicts cost $3,900, and residential treatment cost $6,800. A year of incarceration, on the other hand, cost $25,900, enough to pay for intensive outpatient treatment for ten people.

The Police Foundation of the United Kingdom, a nonprofit organization devoted to improving the efficiency and effectiveness of policing, offered the following report in 2000:

> Our conclusion is that the present law on cannabis produces more harm than it prevents. It is expensive of the time and resources of the criminal justice system and especially of the police. It inevitably bears more heavily on young people in the streets of inner cities, who are also more likely to be from minority ethnic communities, and as such is inimical to police-community relations. It criminalizes large numbers of otherwise law-abiding, mainly young, people to the detriment of their futures . . . and it

inhibits accurate education about the relative risks of different drugs including the risks of cannabis itself.[4]

Legitimate Arguments in Favor of Legalizing Marijuana

Many of the legitimate arguments in favor of legalizing marijuana interlock with one another.

- Marijuana is less injurious physically than the legal drug alcohol.
- Efforts to forcibly control rather than permit the use of marijuana have led to more damage by alienating and incarcerating otherwise law-abiding citizens.
- The government has failed to control the supply of marijuana despite high rates of incarceration for marijuana possession. Since 1975 the percentage of high school seniors who say marijuana is easy to obtain has varied only slightly, between 82 and 86 percent.
- Facing America's drug problem requires a reorientation toward decreasing the demand for drugs. This can be accomplished more effectively through universal access to treatment and educational programs similar to those that have contributed to a decline in tobacco use. By concentrating efforts on trying to reduce the supply of marijuana, we have diverted funds away from treatment of more serious drug addictions (i.e., alcohol, opiates, cocaine, and amphetamine), as well as from the marijuana users who do become addicted.
- Focusing on marijuana as a "gateway" drug, because heroin and crack addicts often experienced pot first, has never made much sense. While 72 million Americans have tried marijuana, only 20 million have ever used cocaine, and fewer than a million are current regular users of cocaine. Similarly, of the millions of

Americans who bought used compact cars as teenagers, some now own BMWs. Were the used compacts "gateway" cars that led to luxury imports later in life? People who enjoy driving often like driving faster and more powerful cars. In the same way, people who like to alter their consciousness with drugs often move on to faster and more powerful drugs. Do the pharmacological effects of marijuana somehow induce people to seek other highs? Or does the discovery that marijuana is not as harmful as the government has claimed and parents have obediently repeated lead people to disregard the warnings about other drugs?

- Several scientific and medical commissions have established the truth about marijuana's relative harmlessness only to have their reports ignored or suppressed. In 1970 the Canadian Le Dain Commission recommended the gradual withdrawal of criminal sanctions against cannabis. In 1972, Richard Nixon's Shafer Commission similarly called for the "decriminalization" of marijuana. Reports commissioned by the British, Canadian, and Dutch governments have also concluded that criminal penalties cause more harm than the drug itself. Since the Dutch decriminalized the retail sale of marijuana by "coffee shops" in 1976, the rate of cannabis use by different age groups has roughly paralleled that in the United States, where severe penalties are credited with preventing wider abuse of pot. In 1988, the DEA's administrative law judge Francis Young heard testimony from dozens of doctors and public health officials before declaring that marijuana should be allowed as medicine. Today the British and Canadian governments are seriously considering following the Dutch by implementing their own version of decriminalizing marijuana.

- The government's choice to permit alcohol is difficult to defend from a purely public health perspective, given that it directly contributes to more than one hundred thousand deaths per year, while there are no deaths recorded as a direct result of marijuana use. The health effects of chronic alcohol use are serious, including increased cancer risk, liver failure from cirrhosis, progressive dementia, and increased mortality from accidents. Alcohol is one of the most toxic chemicals humans use recreationally, adversely affecting every organ of the body. Of all traffic fatalities, 38 percent are alcohol related. A combination of tradition and powerful economic forces continues to promote alcohol as the only legal drug for the purpose of public entertainment, despite its producing serious public health consequences.

- Legalization would permit taxation of marijuana sales, with significant income to the government, some of which could be used to provide treatment for the minority of users who become harmfully involved. Government regulation of growers and sellers would also permit oversight of the drug's purity, as well as providing a means for levying sanctions against those who divert pot to adolescents.

By removing criminal penalties from the use of marijuana, we would reestablish individual freedom and responsibility in an arena the government has never successfully been able to regulate. We would no longer turn otherwise law-abiding citizens into criminals primarily on the basis of their choosing a recreational drug that differs from that preferred by the traditional power structure. And we would end the rhetoric of fear that contaminates drug education today, permitting a more honest approach to the facts about other, more dangerous drugs of abuse.

Legitimate Arguments against Legalizing Marijuana

The arguments against legalizing marijuana are held just as fervently by the opponents of pot.

- Use still equals risk, no matter how persuasively different commissions argue for legalization. Of people over eighteen who begin smoking, 10 percent will eventually become dependent on marijuana, and a progressively higher percent occurs among those who begin smoking marijuana at younger ages. The larger the population that smokes, the more addicts there will be.

- Pot profoundly alters a host of important chemical balances in the brain and physiological functions throughout the body. We now understand that marijuana is addictive, despite centuries of lore to the contrary. The endocannabinoid system is still, in part, a mystery, and caution is warranted in legalizing a drug that stimulates this portion of the brain. As medical researchers better understand the brain's endocannabinoid system, they will refine their search for possible long-term consequences of marijuana use. As with all new drugs being introduced for mass consumption, safety should be established first.

- Cultures take decades, even centuries, to build up shared wisdom about their chosen psychoactive drugs. Introducing or mainstreaming a psychoactive drug to a culture has unpredictable consequences. When a drug is first introduced to a culture, as when the Europeans introduced alcohol to Native Americans and Native Americans introduced tobacco to Europeans, it is often used without control. The annihilation of whole Indian tribes by alcohol is well documented. And it was Europeans who soon used tobacco daily instead of ceremonially. They then found novel ways of inhaling, chewing, and rolling tobacco into cigarettes that enabled constant consumption, all to their detriment.

- Marijuana is a drug of addiction. Even if American culture can integrate marijuana use as successfully as it has alcohol and tobacco (a dubious standard), is it wise to add a psychoactive drug to those that are already legal? Given our experience with Prohibition, the United States is unlikely to prohibit the use of alcohol again, so legalizing marijuana means adding an addictive drug to the list of legal drugs of addiction that are already causing considerable problems. For example, alcohol is involved in one-quarter of all emergency room admissions, one-third of all suicides, and more than half of all homicides and incidents of domestic violence. Alcohol and other drug abuse costs the American economy an estimated $276 billion per year in lost productivity, health care expenditures, crime, motor vehicle crashes, and other conditions.

- The younger generation—the age group for whom pot would not be legal—generally sees marijuana as the drug of choice. Legalizing pot for adults would communicate official acceptance of its use and likely decrease the perception of pot's potential harmfulness. Decriminalization of marijuana in Holland (1976) resulted in use by eighteen- to twenty-year-olds rising from 15 percent in 1984 to 44 percent in 1996, which nearly equals the U.S. rate. Over the past three decades, the primary determinant of whether adolescent marijuana use is rising or falling has been changes in the perception of its harmfulness, not its availability. Sanctioning pot use by adults would inevitably decrease its perception of harmfulness for adolescents as well.

- Pot use complicates the diagnosis and treatment of a variety of underlying psychiatric conditions, from anxiety disorders to depression, ADD, personality disorders, paranoia, and psychosis. Knowing what we do about the potential suffering marijuana can cause people with these conditions, why would we remove a barrier to its use?

- Frequent use of marijuana often impairs maturation psychologically, socially, professionally, and spiritually in adults as well as adolescents, leading to stagnation in their development. Because adolescents are naturally growing far more rapidly than adults, however, the impact of marijuana use is far greater and more immediate. If we cannot restrict alcohol and tobacco to adult use, how can we expect to do a better job with marijuana use? Maintaining the illegal status of marijuana may be experienced as a sacrifice by many adults, but it is a sacrifice worth making to safeguard adolescents.

A decision to legalize marijuana use would represent a massive social experiment by society. The potential negative consequences are significant, especially for young children who would enter their teen years in a radically different environment. Should the social experiment prove unsuccessful, these youngsters would pay the highest price. If current patterns of marijuana use were without problems, perhaps such a social experiment would be justified. Given the reality of adolescent pot use today, however, it is prudent to assume that legalization would only make matters worse.

Public-Health-Oriented Drug Policies: The Alternative to Legalization

Two facts are often ignored in the legalization argument. First, the United States is not going to provide adolescents with legal access to marijuana, just as it does not allow the use of alcohol and tobacco before ages twenty-one and eighteen, respectively. The debate about legalization is *only* a debate about adult use of marijuana. There are pros and cons on each side of the debate regarding adults, and it is unlikely that disaster lurks for adults in either direction we might go.

This is an issue that warrants legitimate debate and democratic resolution. However, no matter which direction we take, we will still have a stake in restricting adolescents' access to marijuana.

The second fact generally ignored by forces opposing legalization is that incarceration is not the only sanction we have for illegal behavior. It is illegal to drive above the speed limit, but only a very small number of people ever get jailed for the offense. Fines, loss of a driver's license, increased insurance premiums, and confinement in weekend driver education programs all converge to control most of our impulses to speed. While incarceration may still be warranted for high-level drug dealers and smugglers, it is hardly the necessary response for possession of small amounts of pot. California voters recently passed a referendum mandating treatment as an alternative to incarceration for nonviolent crimes involving drugs or crimes committed while intoxicated. While the final effects of this fundamental change in policy are not yet known, it is at least a recognition that the state and, by direct extension, its citizens bear full responsibility for any harm that results from its drug policies. The public health approach finds its full expression in Canada's Addiction Research Foundation publication *Cannabis, Health and Public Policy*:

> The use of alcohol, tobacco and other drugs should be seen primarily as a public health issue rather than one dominated by moral or legal principles. The main goal of public policy and practice should be twofold: to reduce harm and cost from drug use, and to minimize the harms and costs of drug policy.[5]

If we eventually choose to permit adults to smoke marijuana legally, we should take care to protect the 10 percent who may someday require treatment by taxing those who sell and purchase marijuana.

This would pool the cost of treatment and share the risk, much as health insurance is intended to do. We would avoid getting into the situation the government currently finds itself in with tobacco companies. Taxpayers bear much of the cost of treating lung cancer and emphysema while the tobacco companies continue to reap profits. And, because it would be an active decision on the part of the government to permit marijuana use, the government would naturally bear some of the responsibility for whatever problems crop up over the next several decades. Taxing consumption and levying licensing fees for those who wish to cultivate their own marijuana would not only protect the government against future liabilities but would also guarantee access to treatment for those who become addicted.

Preventing diversion of marijuana to those under the legal age for marijuana use, whether that would be set at eighteen or twenty-one, would be an important public health issue. In fact, it would probably be an outright public health problem, as it already is today. Perhaps a combination of heavy fines, loss of growing or retail licenses, increased insurance premiums for those doing retail business, and confinement in weekend marijuana education programs for adults who sell to teens would limit teens' access to marijuana. If access became unacceptably easy for adolescents, the policy of legalization for adults would have to be reversed or made more restrictive, a process that could prove exceedingly difficult. Eventually a balance might be reached in which adults would see it as in their own self-interest to keep adolescent access to marijuana at a minimal level, much as they do today with underage driving.

Medical Marijuana

Just as in the debate about legalization of marijuana, we run into a highly politicized, emotionally charged arena when we turn to the debate about medical marijuana—the use of marijuana to treat illness.

If debate requires that each side listen to the other and respond with pertinent arguments, there hasn't been any real debate about whether marijuana has a legitimate role as medication. Instead, the two sides have more often ignored the opposition's facts and dismissed one another as not worthy of a respectful response. If the word *hypocrisy* is used to indicate bad faith, then both sides are guilty of true hypocrisy. Before looking at the legitimate arguments for and against the concept of medical marijuana, it helps to identify the bad faith that each side has displayed for years.

Government Hypocrisy

While the federal government states that additional studies are required before marijuana policies can be changed, reviews of current studies have been carried out and the results repeatedly ignored. The National Commission on Marijuana and Drug Abuse appointed by Richard Nixon published its findings in 1972, *Marijuana: A Signal of Misunderstanding*. Nixon not only ignored the commission's recommendation that pot be decriminalized but led the charge in the opposite direction. He opened further offenses in the War on Drugs, eventually leading to massive increases in the U.S. prison population.

More recently, California (56 to 44 percent) and Arizona (65 to 35 percent) passed referenda in 1996 permitting the use of marijuana as medicine. The White House Office of National Drug Control Policy (ONDCP) responded by asking the Institute of Medicine to conduct a review of the scientific evidence to assess the potential health benefits of the cannabinoids found in marijuana. The report, *Marijuana and Medicine: Assessing the Science Base*, published in 1999, states, "The accumulated data indicate a potential therapeutic value for cannabinoid drugs, particularly for symptoms such as pain, control of nausea and vomiting, and appetite stimulation." The doctors recommended that "clinical trials of cannabinoid drugs for symptom management should be conducted with the goal of developing rapid-onset, reliable, and safe delivery systems."

Following passage of the medical marijuana referendum in California, Barry McCaffrey, director of the Office of National Drug Control Policy (also known as the White House drug czar), said in a 1996 press release: "There could be no worse message to young people. . . . Just when the nation is trying its hardest to educate teenagers not to use psychoactive drugs, now they are being told that marijuana is medicine." The Institute of Medicine addressed this concern in its report, saying:

> There is a broad social concern that sanctioning use of marijuana might increase its use among the general population. At this point there are no convincing data to support this concern. The existing data are consistent with the idea that this would not be a problem if the medicinal use of marijuana were as closely regulated as other medications with abuse potential.

The DEA, speaking for the federal government, continues to claim that marijuana has *no accepted medical use and represents a high abuse potential.* Is the federal government operating in good faith, or is it rigidly adhering to established policies out of fear of political fallout from acknowledging their inadequacy?

The Hypocrisy of Medical Marijuana Advocates

The California and Arizona referenda were supported by an odd alliance. Out-of-state billionaires financed the campaigns, largely out of a desire to reform drug laws that criminalize and incarcerate users. Legalization advocates organized under the banner of compassion and medical necessity. Ordinary citizens, Republicans and Democrats alike, who had watched aging parents suffering from cancer, were ready to provide ill family members with whatever solace they could find. Added to this was the powerful gay community, who had witnessed the wholesale decimation of their ranks by AIDS. When pot was seen to help alleviate the horrible wasting seen in their friends and lovers, they strongly backed the referenda as well. Civil libertarians contributed to the alliance out of their philosophical support for individual freedom from government regulation. Several members of the medical community also raised their voices in support of medical marijuana. In the end, the vote in favor of permitting medical marijuana probably had as much to do with giving people an opportunity to strike a blow against the failed heavy hand of the War on Drugs as it did with its proven benefits as a medicine.

But a barely hidden agenda lay behind much of the support for medical marijuana. Like a camel's nose poking under the tent, the intent of many referenda supporters was to establish a beachhead in the campaign to fully legalize marijuana. For example, advocates of medical marijuana such as Dennis Peron, director of San Francisco's Cannabis Cultivators Club, openly flouted laws outlawing marijuana. Quoted as saying, "All marijuana use is medicinal," Peron appears to feel no caution about the potential for addiction and seems intent on making pot available to everyone who wants it. Images of "patients" joyfully lighting up in his center's party atmosphere have frequently been broadcast on local television news. At least two of my patients in recovery have been so stimulated by the images that they relapsed.

How many of the advocates of medical marijuana are operating in good faith? How many are ignoring evidence of marijuana's addictive potential and high risk for adolescents in their drive to legalize all marijuana use?

The Medical Potential for Cannabinoids

The focus needs to be shifted from marijuana to the endocannabinoid system in our brains. The question science needs to address is whether increasing or decreasing activity within this system would have benefits in the treatment of any illnesses. We already treat some illnesses (schizophrenia and parkinsonism) by modifying brain levels of the neurotransmitter dopamine. We treat depression and obsessive-compulsive disorder by modifying levels of another neurotransmitter, serotonin. It certainly seems reasonable that modifying activity in the endocannabinoid system, *if* this can be done without incurring an unacceptable level of side effects, could produce some benefits. Ralph Mechoulam, the discoverer of THC's structure and the endocannabinoid anandamide, believes that the brain's cannabinoid network is involved in several different physiological processes that could be influenced medically to help with pain management, memory formation, appetite, the coordination of movement, and possibly even emotion. Additional medical research should eventually find ways to increase or decrease the level of naturally occurring endocannabinoids or to modify cannabinoid molecules in ways that increase their beneficial effects while eliminating current side effects.

The cannabinoid system has the exciting potential for providing a whole array of new medications for the control of pain. Patients requiring morphine for chronic pain find that they need less if THC is added to their treatment. Research has also shown that animals are less sensitive to painful stimuli (e.g., placing their tails on a hot plate) when first given THC. Brain researchers now see the endorphin and cannabinoid systems as two independent but *parallel* and *overlapping* physiological regulatory systems. Both are involved in controlling our sensitivity to pain.

As noted in chapter 2, cannabinoids are richly concentrated in the hippocampus, the seat of memory formation. By blocking cannabinoid activity, memory can be improved in older rats. Scientists have also been able to genetically engineer mice that are born with no cannabinoid receptors. These mice, with zero cannabinoid activity in the brain, have been shown to have better memory than normal mice. Mice that lack any cannabinoid activity remember negative events longer than normal, perhaps revealing that one of the functions of a healthy endocannabinoid system is to reduce the impact of negative events. Will we someday develop new treatments for memory loss, including the effects of Alzheimer's disease, by modifying cannabinoid activity in the hippocampus?

Appetite loss, with resultant muscle wasting, is a consistent complication in cancer and AIDS. Research has now confirmed that THC can stimulate appetite, with important reversal of the wasting syndrome that weakens patients so terribly. Cancer doctors have also found repeatedly that smoked marijuana does control nausea and vomiting in the 10 to 20 percent of chemotherapy patients who are not otherwise helped by current antinausea medications. The value of inhaling medication for nausea is that its effectiveness does not rely on being able to keep a pill down. If, at the same time, the THC diminishes memory for the noxious experience of chemotherapy, this would be merciful, too. On the other hand, cancer patients who have never previously experienced marijuana generally find the mental side effects to be unpleasant.

The high number of cannabinoid receptor sites in motor areas of the brain (basal ganglia and cerebellum) causes spontaneous motor activity to be quelled when stimulated by THC. Many people suffering from the spasticity and tremors of multiple sclerosis and spinal cord injury have experienced benefit from increasing activity at these receptors. Individuals have shown a markedly increased ability to draw a straight line (as opposed to a jagged, saw-toothed pattern) with as little as five milligrams of THC. When spasticity interferes with sleep, the sedating effect of THC is doubly useful, although it does cause some disturbance in sleeping brain waves. In some multiple sclerosis patients, THC also improves bladder control, decreasing the need to interrupt sleep for frequent urination.

The modification of mood is a very delicate affair. Although some people claim that THC acts as a useful antidepressant, these claims have to be balanced against the possibility that its ongoing use is simply preventing the irritability of withdrawal. It is also quite common for people to report that their depression clears after stopping marijuana use. THC currently fails to meet one of the primary criteria used to evaluate effective antidepressants—transparency. While people may be willing to tolerate some mental side effects when they are using a cannabinoid medication to prevent the nausea of chemotherapy, we strive to make antidepressants as transparent as vitamins. No one feels "vitaminized" in the afternoon from taking a multivitamin at breakfast, and effective antidepressants generally have minimal mental side effects. Case in point—street addicts don't pay money to get high on Prozac. If cannabinoid molecules are ever modified to have far fewer psychological effects, it will make sense to test them for antidepressant qualities.

In summary, there is more than enough hard evidence that modifying our brain's cannabinoid activity, up and down, has potential benefit in a variety of illnesses to warrant the rapid development of more effective, safer medications.

Legitimate Arguments against Medical Marijuana

By now it should be clear that the real issue is not marijuana itself, but rather the helpfulness of blocking or increasing the brain's normal cannabinoid activity. Marijuana just happens to be the first means humans have discovered for accomplishing this neurochemical manipulation. In the same way, the poppy plant's production of opiates led us to discover the mercy of morphine and then the brain's endorphin system. Tree bark led us to discover aspirin and antimalarial medications. The foxglove plant first gave us digitalis for the treatment of heart failure. But we don't brew foxglove tea today. How would we control the dose? And why wouldn't we use the much more effective pharmaceutical forms of digitalis that are now available?

The American Medical Association put it clearly in Report 10, a 1997 text on medical marijuana:

> The concept of burning and inhaling the combustion products of a dried plant . . . containing dozens of toxins and carcinogenic chemicals as a therapeutic agent represents a significant departure from the standard drug approval process. According to this viewpoint, legitimate therapeutic agents are comprised of a purified substance(s) that can be manufactured and tested in a reproducible way.

This is the tradition of modern medicine, to extract the essence of plants, then to purify and alter it until the side effects are minimized and the effectiveness is increased. The idea of sucking the hot ashes from a burning plant into the depths of the lungs is already an anachronism.

Marijuana smoke is similar in chemical composition to tobacco smoke, except that it contains THC rather than nicotine. Each joint deposits four to five times more tar in the lungs than a tobacco cigarette and results in a fivefold greater increase in carbon monoxide absorbed. Because marijuana smoke is inhaled one-third deeper and is held in the lungs four times longer, three to four joints are equivalent to more than twenty tobacco cigarettes. Approximately the same percentage of tobacco and marijuana smokers (20 percent) report symptoms of chronic bronchitis.[6] While there is no final scientific proof that marijuana causes cancer, hard evidence linking tobacco and cancer required decades of huge studies. Such studies have not been undertaken with pot. However, the presence in marijuana smoke of the same carcinogenic compounds found in tobacco smoke argues in favor of assuming a cancer risk exists until proved otherwise.

It is interesting that cigarettes used to be touted for their health-promoting qualities. As recently as the 1950s, doctors appeared in advertisements proclaiming the soothing properties of name brands. Extreme caution is appropriate whenever we suspect that the potential harmful effects of any medication are being downplayed. As Hanna Rosin wrote in the *New Republic*, "Pot may be medicine, but getting high every day is still getting high every day."[7]

Furthermore, it is impossible to control the dose of THC obtained from a joint or to control for whatever other plant products and pesticides may also be present. Quality control is absent in the current use of medical marijuana.

Moving beyond the Hype

When California was about to vote on the medical marijuana referendum in 1996, I expressed distress to my colleagues in the California Society of Addiction Medicine that we had not developed any public position on the issue. Thus began my sojourn into this arena, as I was appointed to head a task force that fairly represented the membership to study the scientific literature. Personally, I thought that the idea of any medical usefulness for pot was a joke.

The literature doesn't permit this ignorant opinion to last for long. Once we understand that the brain, not the cannabis plant, is the source of wonder, it becomes apparent that cannabinoid medicines designed to alter our brain's normal activity are highly likely. The question is which diseases these alterations will benefit and whether medications can be produced that are reliable, safe, and effective. The question of smoking marijuana as the primary avenue for delivering a drug that can alter our brain's cannabinoid activity will quickly become as outmoded as chewing tree bark to get the benefit of aspirin. We need to release the scientific and medical community to do what it does best—to extract, purify, and modify cannabinoids and to test them rigorously. Continuing to permit law enforcement to determine which drugs are appropriate to be used as medications is an unnecessary limitation to our freedom and a barrier to scientific progress.

The argument that medical marijuana increases the risk that adolescents will be encouraged to smoke recreationally may be true, as long as they see images of people getting high in the partylike atmosphere of some cannabis clubs on television news. However, no one argues that the legitimate use of morphine encourages teens to use heroin. The medical community already possesses the framework for beneficially employing drugs that are far more addictive and dangerous than marijuana. Dangerously addictive drugs, such as morphine, are more tightly controlled by the DEA than are other medications, primarily through the process of triplicate prescriptions. Triplicates enable the DEA to keep tabs on physicians' prescribing practices. Any doctor who is running a "pill mill" will come to the DEA's attention and be investigated.

When opiate medications need to be used on an ongoing basis for chronic pain or when antianxiety medications such as Valium are required for extended periods of time, addiction becomes a possibility. Presumably, cannabinoid medications could also produce addiction, especially in the ongoing treatment of conditions such as the spasticity and tremor of multiple sclerosis. In cases where physicians are prescribing potentially addictive medications, they are obligated to assure that they have obtained a patient's informed consent. The risk and consequences of addiction need to be explained sufficiently for patients to share in the decision that the medication has enough probable benefit to use, despite its potential for addiction. Physicians are obliged to monitor whether the medication is being taken properly and continues to be effective. Pain management is an issue for addicts in recovery, many of whom follow strict guidelines and use their support systems when they decide that taking an addictive substance is the lesser of two evils. Similar monitoring of cannabinoid medications would minimize the risks inherent in their use.

The problem with referenda permitting the use of medical marijuana is that they have not truly medicalized marijuana. For example, the California Medical Board requires that medications, especially those with a potential for abuse or damaging side effects, be prescribed by a physician only within the following context:

- a good-faith history and physical
- a treatment plan, with diagnosis and goals
- informed consent
- periodic reviews of effectiveness
- proper records

By creating a framework outside the medical field that permits physicians to "recommend" but not prescribe marijuana, California's referendum has essentially masked the uncontrolled distribution of marijuana under a pseudomedical cloak. But it has failed to give the physicians the freedom or the responsibility for treating this drug like any other medicine of equal potential for either help or harm.

Concluding Remarks

The legalization of marijuana is a decision to be made democratically, after thorough public debate. If legalization were to be undertaken with sufficient safeguards against increasing access to pot by adolescents, it would be unlikely to create the chaos and disaster predicted by its opponents. The Dutch experience provides a useful guide in coming to this nonalarmist conclusion. The basic reality, however, is that public health concerns will almost certainly provide sufficient arguments to keep marijuana away from the high-risk groups represented by children and teens. Therefore, complete legalization of marijuana, permitting adolescents uncontrolled access, is unlikely ever to exist, just as it does not exist for tobacco and alcohol.

Some form of decriminalizing marijuana may well serve as a useful intermediate step in rethinking America's self-destructive War on Drugs. By allowing treatment and demand reduction to take the place of incarceration and supply reduction, our society could reap several benefits almost immediately. Those in need of medical care as the result of having become dependent on marijuana would be more likely to receive help. Those who are currently imprisoned for marijuana possession alone would no longer be criminalized, alienated, and stigmatized. Prison costs would drop substantially, and government resources available for drug control could be more effectively focused on drugs such as cocaine, methamphetamine, and heroin. By decriminalizing people who smoke marijuana, we would begin a complete rethinking of the War on Drugs.

The medical use of cannabinoids originally derived from the cannabis plant is very likely to occur. The basis of this prediction lies in the brain's own natural chemistry, which can be modified in a variety of potentially useful ways by drugs that stimulate and block the endocannabinoid neural network. We cannot yet be sure how important these medications will eventually prove to be, although there is some legitimate hope that new methods for controlling pain will become possible. The addition of new analgesic drugs has the potential for extensive value. It is highly unlikely, however, that inhaled marijuana smoke will ever be taken seriously by most physicians, especially after more advanced cannabinoid medications become available. On the other hand, there may well be a role for quick-acting aerosol forms of cannabinoid medications, because this delivery system provides a high level of control over dose regulation, in the same way that morphine pumps permit patients to titrate doses more swiftly and accurately than oral tablets.

Concluding Thoughts: An Open Letter

To Parents

Life has a way of not always going according to plan. Sometimes our professional lives wriggle off in directions we never anticipated. Our health may fail in unexpected ways. And often our children do not follow our lead very well. They do not match up to our early dreams or share our goals and interests as much as we had hoped. They are separate beings from their birthdays on, soon pursuing their own paths. We want desperately to protect them from being hurt, without smothering them with our fears. It is a balance that often eludes most of us.

When we watch marijuana enter our child's world, most of us feel left on the other side of a divide from a son or daughter. Suddenly, fear grips our hearts. Those of us who enjoyed pot during our younger years may feel hypocritical in our caution. We may feel inexplicably more conservative than we had ever imagined we could. Nevertheless, the love that connects our soul to our child's is elemental. We want only what is best for our flesh and blood and have difficulty tolerating what little control we have over their world.

Our children's brains are one of the most complex things in the universe, fragile organs from which their minds somehow emerge. Laced throughout these delicate brains are a host of nerves that

237

naturally produce and use cannabinoid molecules to regulate memory, the ability to sense novelty, sensitivity to pain, and the ability to rest quietly. Driving the brain far from its normal chemical balance by flooding it with the mimicry of THC may be an experience 90 percent of adults can more or less tolerate, but adolescents may react differently. Adults are no longer in the middle of their mental, emotional, and social development, while adolescents are squarely in the middle of one of the most important developmental periods of their lives. The tragic results of derailing this development with pot are predictable for too many teens.

As much as we want to protect our children, we must learn to tolerate the risks they have to take in order to grow. Because teens are often still incapable of being realistic about the risks they are taking, the responsibility for recognizing when a child has spun out of control with marijuana also rests on our shoulders. It is understandable that we fear marijuana and feel despair when we see our child's spirit slipping away.

As parents, we are challenged to move beyond ourselves. We need to abandon our cherished opinions about marijuana in order to acknowledge new scientific understandings. We need to go beyond our prejudices about addiction in order to learn more effective ways of approaching our child's problems. We need to shed the blame and guilt and the moralizing and pontificating that we are all capable of in order to have open ears and clear eyes. We need to move beyond ourselves in ways that are often painful, almost always unwelcome, but eventually very much to everyone's benefit. We have to find the honesty to admit that our love is not sufficient to guide youngsters toward maturity without the willingness to set boundaries. Our compassion for a child is useless, and even harmful, when it diminishes the ability to tolerate his or her anger and deep resentment as we draw a line around unacceptable behavior.

Some of us have to get out of ourselves in order to stop trying to control our children. We have to recognize our limited ability to force others to behave or to see the world the way we do. We have to accept that we can be defied. No amount of anger or will can make children think the thoughts we want them to have or feel the emotions we believe are best. No amount of shaming can create a healthier child, only a more defeated or a more defiant one.

Others of us have to get out of ourselves in order to stop trying to bribe or coddle our children in the vain hope that they will somehow survive and eventually mature. Vague faith that God will give our children only what they are ready to handle, that everyone is on his or her own path, and that freedom is the ultimate gift we can bestow on the next generation are philosophies that may soothe us. But freedom has to be earned if it is going to be more than license. Our children depend on us to accept the responsibility of establishing a balance between setting limits and letting go, allowing the natural consequences of their choices to unfold and guide them.

To Teens

Being part of a family and a community is like finding yourself in an immense parade, one that began before anyone can remember. At first we are carried in the parade by our parents, then pushed in a stroller, and eventually we walk along on our own. At some point down the road we may have to push our parents in their wheelchairs for a way. Eventually we carry them for a block or two before they leave the parade forever. Then we rejoin the growing mass of marching people and head on as far as we are able. When we are gone, too, the parade will continue into a future we can only imagine. Before we were born, our family was there. After we are gone, family will endure. It is far larger than each one of us.

Family tries to give you safety. It tries to protect you against disease and injury, when possible. It tries to protect you against the scorn and uncaring of the world, when possible. It tries to keep the dangers of the world in perspective and dispel the cold that can creep into people's hearts when they are too much alone.

Too often families have been so wounded that they become the source of danger for children. Hurt people often can hurt other people, even little people. But even when those we expect to love us can't, we never stop needing someone to treat us as family. The need is so deep that most of us keep looking until we find someone to accept and soothe us as only family can.

Family does all this in two ways: by the love, honesty, and loyalty of its members and by creating a beacon that points the way through life. This beacon is the set of values that define each family—the standards, the morals, and the ideals that each family holds dear.

Your health and safety is one of the most important of those values. Family will fight to protect you against whatever they see threatening your health and safety, even when it is your own behavior that is the biggest threat. The use of marijuana during your teen years entails risk. The younger you begin smoking pot, the greater the risk. If your parents believe you are harming yourself and jeopardizing your future with marijuana, they have an obligation to you, to themselves, and to your family as a whole. They will do whatever they deem necessary to protect your health and safety. You would do nothing less for your own children. If today you do not see the love and loyalty that guides your parents, you may resent them. That is natural. But do not expect that to stop them.

You are more precious to the family than you may understand.

The Twelve Steps of Alcoholics Anonymous*

1. We admitted we were powerless over alcohol—that our lives had become unmanageable.
2. Came to believe that a Power greater than ourselves could restore us to sanity.
3. Made a decision to turn our will and our lives over to the care of God *as we understood Him*.
4. Made a searching and fearless moral inventory of ourselves.
5. Admitted to God, to ourselves, and to another human being the exact nature of our wrongs.
6. Were entirely ready to have God remove all these defects of character.
7. Humbly asked Him to remove our shortcomings.
8. Made a list of all persons we had harmed, and became willing to make amends to them all.
9. Made direct amends to such people wherever possible, except when to do so would injure them or others.
10. Continued to take personal inventory and when we were wrong promptly admitted it.
11. Sought through prayer and meditation to improve our conscious contact with God *as we understood Him*, praying only for knowledge of His will for us and the power to carry that out.
12. Having had a spiritual awakening as the result of these steps, we tried to carry this message to alcoholics, and to practice these principles in all our affairs.

---

*The Twelve Steps of AA are taken from *Alcoholics Anonymous*, 4th ed., published by AA World Services, New York, N.Y., 59–60. Reprinted with permission of AA World Services. (See author's note on copyright page.)

The Twelve Steps of Marijuana Anonymous*

1. We admitted we were powerless over marijuana, that our lives had become unmanageable.
2. Came to believe that a Power greater than ourselves could restore us to sanity.
3. Made a decision to turn our will and our lives over to the care of God, as we understood God.
4. Made a searching and fearless moral inventory of ourselves.
5. Admitted to God, to ourselves, and to another human being the exact nature of our wrongs.
6. Were entirely ready to have God remove all these defects of character.
7. Humbly asked God to remove our shortcomings.
8. Made a list of all persons we had harmed, and became willing to make amends to them all.
9. Made direct amends to such people wherever possible, except when to do so would injure them or others.
10. Continued to take personal inventory and when we were wrong, promptly admitted it.
11. Sought through prayer and meditation to improve our conscious contact with God, as we understood God, praying only for knowledge of God's will for us and the power to carry that out.
12. Having had a spiritual awakening as the result of these steps, we tried to carry this message to marijuana addicts and to practice these principles in all our affairs.

---

*The Twelve Steps of Marijuana Anonymous are adapted with permission of AA World Services and reprinted with permission of MA World Services, Inc. (See author's note on copyright page.)

Notes

Chapter 1: Cannabis: Putting Pot into Perspective

1. U.S. Department of Health and Human Services, Centers for Disease Control and Prevention, National Center for Chronic Disease Prevention and Health Promotion, "Targeting Tobacco Use: The Nation's Leading Cause of Death." Available on-line at www.cdc.gov/nccdphp/aag/aag_osh.htm.

2. National Council on Alcoholism and Drug Dependence, "Alcoholism and Alcohol-Related Problems: A Sobering Look." Available on-line at ncadd.org/facts/problems.html.

3. Ibid.

Chapter 3: Marijuana Addiction? What Is the Evidence?

1. Andrew Weil and Winifred Rosen, *From Chocolate to Morphine* (Boston: Houghton Mifflin, 1993), 25–26.

Chapter 4: Why Teens Begin Using Marijuana: The Seductive Power of Pot

1. Carl Sagan, "Mr. X." Available on-line at marijuana-uses.com/examples/Mr_X.htm.

Chapter 5: High-Risk Teens: The Unequal Distribution of Risk

1. *'Pass It On': The Story of Bill Wilson and How the A.A. Message Reached the World* (New York: Alcoholics Anonymous World Services, Inc., 1984), 56.

2. A. Troisi et al., "Psychiatric Symptoms in Male Cannabis Users Not Using Other Illicit Drugs," *Addiction* 93 (April 1998): 487–92.

Chapter 9: Treatment: What to Expect

1. U.S. Department of Health and Human Services, National Institutes of Health, National Institute on Drug Abuse, "Marijuana Abuse," Research Report Series (October 2002). NIH publication number 02-3859.

2. Andrew Weil, *The Natural Mind: How the Relationship between Mind and Body Suggests a Revolutionary Approach to the Drug Problem* (Boston: Houghton Mifflin, 1972), 97.

Chapter 10: Recovery: Healthy Mind, Body, and Spirit
1. A beautiful description of the wisdom contained in the Twelve Steps can be found in Ernest and Katherine Ketcham, *The Spirituality of Imperfection* (New York: Bantam Books, 1992).

Chapter 11: Prevention: Philosophies and Protective Factors
1. Conducted by the Division of Epidemiology, School of Public Health, University of Minnesota, under funding from the National Institute of Alcohol Abuse and Alcoholism (NIAAA) of the National Institutes of Health (NIH) (www.epi.umn.edu/projectnorthland/default.html).
2. Weil and Rosen, *From Chocolate to Morphine*, 3–5.
3. Weil, *The Natural Mind*, xii.
4. Weil and Rosen, *From Chocolate to Morphine*, 2.

Chapter 12: Current Debates about Marijuana: Cutting through the Rhetoric
1. Dan Baum, *Smoke and Mirrors: The War on Drugs and the Politics of Failure* (Boston: Little Brown, 1996), 7.
2. Ibid., 12
3. Ibid., 233.
4. Police Foundation of the United Kingdom, *Drugs and the Law: Report of the Independent Inquiry into the Misuse of Drugs Act 1971*. Available on-line at www.druglibrary.org/schaffer/library/studies/runciman/default.htm.
5. *Cannabis, Health and Public Policy* (Toronto: Addiction Research Foundation, 1997). Available on-line at sano.camh.net/announce/n_a9801h.htm.
6. British Lung Foundation, "A Smoking Gun? The Impact of Cannabis Smoking on Respiratory Health." Available on-line at www.lunguk.org/cannabis/a_smoking_gun.pdf.
7. Hanna Rosin, "The Return of Pot," *New Republic*, 17 February 1997, 111–17.

Index

About the Author

Timmen L. Cermak, M.D., studied philosophy at Ohio Wesleyan University before graduating from Case Western Reserve Medical School in 1972. After two years with the Indian Health Service, he completed his psychiatry residency at Stanford University, where he assisted Dr. Stephanie Brown in creating the first therapy group for adult children of alcoholics. Following a postdoctoral fellowship in neurophysiology under Dr. Karl Pribram, he served as medical director of the alcohol inpatient unit at the San Francisco Veterans Administration Hospital from 1982 to 1985. During this time he helped found the National Association for Children of Alcoholics (NACoA), serving first as president and then chairman of the board. Dr. Cermak is Board Certified in Psychiatry, with a Certificate of Added Qualification in Addiction Psychiatry. A member of the California Society of Addiction Medicine (CSAM), he chaired CSAM's task force on medical marijuana (1996 to 2000). Dr. Cermak is also a member of the American Academy of Addiction Psychiatry (AAAP). He is the author of *Diagnosing and Treating Co-dependence*, *A Time to Heal*, and *Evaluating and Treating Adult Children of Alcoholics*. He is in private practice in the San Francisco Bay area.